PENNSYLVANIA

1681—1756

The State without an Army

FIRST PUBLISHED: 1937

PENNSYLVANIA

1681—1756

The State without an Army

By

E. DINGWALL and E. A. HEARD

*A Study in Eight Chapters
and Four Appendices*

LONDON:

THE C. W. DANIEL COMPANY LTD.

40 GREAT RUSSELL STREET, W.C.1

MADE AND PRINTED
IN GREAT BRITAIN

"It equally concerns men in every age to take heed
to their own spirit."

John Woolman

FOREWORD

THIS is not a biography of William Penn. The dramatic story of "the Admiral's son turned Quaker" has been told by writers of many nations from many points of view, one of the most recent being a work for Swedish readers. (*William Penn en bok om samvete och stat* (a book on conscience and State) by Dr. Emilia Fogelklou, Stockholm, 1935.)

Still less does it claim to be a history of Pennsylvania. It is an attempt to group together certain recognised facts with relation to their historical and geographical background and their significance to-day. It is also an attempt to examine a body of principles with their outworking under a peculiar set of conditions, in order to gain light on the international problems of our age.

"The wisdom of former ages when transmitted in writing to posterity is an inestimable treasure" are the opening words of Robert Proud's *History of Pennsylvania*.

This short study does not claim to be more than an outline of an historic period. Doubtless it could have been much more if the documents and records in America had been consulted. It is an attempt to collect the facts in so far as they are available on this side of the Atlantic, and to record them truly and consecutively. It is also an endeavour to answer in some measure the questions: Did Penn's experiment succeed or fail? If the former, to what extent? If the latter, for what reasons?"

5

My thanks are here expressed to all who have contributed in any way towards the production and completion of the work. My brother, Dr. E. J. Dingwall, of Cambridge, has given time and thought in making valuable criticisms and in suggesting lines of research. I wish to thank John L. Nickalls for making available to me the volumes of the Friends' Reference Library at Friends' House, and especially for his kindness in reading and correcting the manuscript and for making notes therein. My thanks are due to Mr. W. H. S. Roberts, the Librarian of the Weston-super-Mare Free Library for his help in obtaining information and for making it possible for me to consult many works of reference. In this connection, acknowledgment must be made also to the members of the staff of the Cambridge University Library and of the Library of the British Museum. Further, I wish to express gratitude and appreciation to all authors and publishers who have given the necessary permission for quotations to be made from their works. My friend Elizabeth Ann Heard, has entered so deeply into the spirit of the work and has rendered such invaluable assistance that, but for her help, the manuscript in its present form would never have existed. Lastly, I wish to record that my source of inspiration has been found in the life and work for many years of the Weston-super-Mare Peace Society in general, and of its Honorary Secretary in particular. Without it, this book would never have been written.

E. DINGWALL.

BLEADON, SOMERSET.
August 15th, 1937.

CONTENTS

PENNSYLVANIA

1681—1756

The State without an Army

Chapter I

THE FOUNDER OF PENNSYLVANIA

WILLIAM PENN, son of Vice-Admiral Penn and Margaret Van der Schuren, daughter of John Jasper, of County Clare, was born in London, October 14th, 1644. At this time George Fox, son of a weaver and twenty years of age, was wandering about England in his search for Truth. The admiral being much at sea, young Penn was brought up quietly by his mother at Chigwell, Essex, where he attended the village church and the free grammar school. His uncle, George Penn, a merchant in Spain, was then suffering greatly under the Inquisition, and it has been suggested that the boy learned thereby "to loathe the practices of a persecuting Church."[1]

It is on record that when about eleven years old he had a strange spiritual experience. "Alone in his chamber, 'he was suddenly surprised with an inward comfort; and, as he thought, an external glory in the room, which gave rise to religious emotions, during which he had the strongest conviction of the being of a God, and that the Soul of man was capable of enjoying communication with Him. He believed also that the seal of Divinity had been put upon him at this

[1] W. Hepworth Dixon. *History of William Penn. Founder of Pennsylvania.* London, 1872 (p. 28).

moment, or that he had been awakened or called upon to a holy life.' "[1]

A year later the Penn family moved to Ireland, to occupy a fortified castle at Macroom. By this time (1656) George Fox had created a powerful movement in England, which was spreading to Ireland. Admiral Penn, wishing to hear the Quaker message, invited Thomas Loe, a tradesman from Oxford, then preaching at Cork, to visit Macroom. This inspired apostle aroused deep emotions in the young, sensitive lad, whose reasoning led him to ponder "What if we should all be Quakers?" There being no one similarly interested with whom to discuss his inward queryings, he dwelt much upon Loe's words which called to mind his earlier spiritual experience. He wrote: "I am a child alone," and in later life he confessed "I never had any religion than what I felt, except a little profession that came with education"[2] and again, "The knowledge of God from the Living Witness from thirteen years of age hath been dear to me."[3]

In 1660, when Penn was sixteen, he was sent to Christ Church, Oxford, where much religious conflict was rife. Dr. John Owen, Thomas Loe and others were influencing men's minds against the ritual of the Church. Penn became involved, and some 'disgraceful' scenes occurred, in which the young man clearly showed his tendencies towards the Quaker way of life. His father, now a knight, was bitterly disappointed at such a choice. In the hope of curing his son of this

---

[1] J. Stoughton. *William Penn. The Founder of Pennsylvania.* London, 1882 (p. 8).

[2] Bonamy Dobrée. *William Penn. Quaker and Pioneer.* London, 1932 (p. 13).

[3] C. E. Vulliamy. *William Penn.* London, 1933 (p. 35).

Quakerism he arranged a "grand tour" for him—first to France, thence to Italy. At the Huguenot college at Saumur, he came under the influence of a powerful, scholarly mind, embodying the ideals of religious liberty, that of Moise Amyraut, who taught him concerning early Church doctrines and the history of religious controversy. His spiritual perceptions, too, were growing: in a contretemps with a would-be antagonist in a Paris street he had disarmed instead of fighting his opponent.

However, on his return to England, he brought with him many worldly impressions of Paris with its gaiety. But the outbreak of plague which occurred during his study of law at Lincoln's Inn in 1665, brought to him a realisation of "the Vanity of this World and the Irreligiousness of the Religious of it."[1] Sir William, fearing a return to the more austere religion, and hoping to encourage the development of the least trace of worldly social activity in his son, soon seized an opportunity of sending him to Ireland. Certain estates there were temporarily occupied by Colonel Wallis (granted to him by Cromwell); later these were granted by the King to Sir William. To get possession of them required much legal skill, tact, and diplomacy. Young William Penn showed astounding ability: he succeeded not only in winning them, but later in managing them most satisfactorily. He was soon revelling in every mode of 'life' in Dublin at the Viceregal Lodge, the extremely brilliant entourage of the Duke of Ormonde, then Lord Lieutenant. A friendship was established which led to Penn's volunteering to accompany the

[1] Mabel R. Brailsford. *William Penn*. Friends' Tract Association, London, 1934 (p. 13).

Duke's son on active service to quell a mutiny at
Carrickfergus. The glamour of this military exploit
tempted him to consider Ormonde's offer of a captaincy.
He even went so far as to have his portrait painted in
armour. Hence "the single record which the world
possesses of a man whose name is Peace displays him
in a coat of shining steel."[1] His own father, however,
was the unconscious instrument of leading him into
still further opportunities for a religious life by refusing
to give his consent to the son's appeal to be granted a
military title. Baulked of his ambition, William
returned to the Shangarry estates near Cork. Here at
this very time Thomas Loe was again preaching to
Friends. Penn was already feeling a renewed yearning
to learn more of the principles of life as set forth by
such teachers. He went joyfully to Loe's meeting and
heard his exposition of the formula: "There is a faith
which overcometh the world, and there is a faith which
is overcome by the world," and he knew from that
moment which way of life he would follow. "I was
directed to the testimony of Jesus in mine own conscience,"[2] he says of himself after this experience.
Deeply impressed by the eloquence and sincerity of
the speaker, he was moved to examine his own heart,
and it seemed to him that the light of the Spirit of
Truth was given him, and that "he rose into another
sphere of spiritual life and consciousness."[3] He became
"William Penn whom divine love constrains . . . having
beheld the majesty of Him Who is invisible,"[4] and

[1] Dixon. Op. cit., p. 43.
[2] Dobrée. Op. cit., p. 33.
[3] Stoughton. Op. cit., p. 46.
[4] Quoted from *Truth Exalted* (W. Penn) by W. H. Dixon. Op. cit.,
p. 57.

thenceforth he "hung up his sword and coat of mail, and put into a trunk his lace and plume."[1] He had put away for ever the regular social life of his day, and had definitely ranked himself on the side of those who stood for righteousness and a religion embodying the principle of love. These men were proving to be problems in nearly every accepted mode of living. Cromwell could not deal with their non-resistance; one could not make soldiers out of men who would not fight nor run away; nor could he control men who raised no opposition to whatever he did to them. He had to realise that the man of love was the man of power. Followers of George Fox were men who would not be coerced by human authority—they believed in "the inward, independent, indestructible, light in every human soul";[2] their conscience must be sacrosanct; they refused to show reverence by baring their heads to any man, whatever his status, for to them all men were equal; only to God could such homage be paid. They would not conform to the religious rites and ceremonial of the Church and detested its casuistries; theirs was the Church universal. "They declined to pay tithes . . . took no oaths . . . drank no healths."[3] Each man felt a power in his own being—enabling him to conduct his life as the spirit prompted, and uniting him with all others who hearkened to the same voice within.

Very soon Penn was to show publicly to what state of mind he had grown. At a Friends' Meeting in Cork, soldiers caused a disturbance with a view to ending the meeting. The young enthusiast forcibly ejected the leader. This led to his imprisonment, where, in contrite

---

[1] Ib., p. 55.   [2] Dixon. Op. cit., p. 53.
[3] Samuel M. Janney. *Life of William Penn.* Philadelphia, 1882 (p. 49).

mood and full of desire to rectify his mistake, he wrote
a considered letter to the Lord President of Munster,
showing the right of every man to obey his own
conscience. Release followed immediately.

His Quaker opinions and mannerisms irritated his
father beyond measure. In spite of a real devotion to
one another, the elder Penn grew so enraged at his
son's 'thee and thou'-ing (as he called it) even such
persons as the King, the Duke of York and himself,
that he turned him out of his house. This was in
London, in 1667. His ardour was by no means lessened
by this—rather it provoked in him an intention to
further the cause by becoming a minister in the Society
and a writer. His first effort, *Truth Exalted*, was published in 1668; the next work, a tract called *The Sandy
Foundation Shaken*, aimed directly at Thomas Vincent
and his followers, led to his imprisonment in the Tower
of London under exceedingly harsh and restrictive
conditions. During his seven or eight months of confinement he wrote his well-known book *No Cross, no
Crown*. On his release in 1669 he immediately set to
work to get all imprisoned Quakers in Ireland given
their liberty. This achieved, he returned to London.

The year 1670 witnessed one of the most famous
trials known to history: that of William Penn and
William Mead, who were arrested in London on an
indictment "that they did unlawfully and tumultously
assemble . . . to the great disturbance of" His Majesty's
peace. The two Friends arriving at Gracechurch
Street to join others in their Meeting for worship found
the house guarded by soldiers. Admittance was
refused them. Penn thereupon turned about and began
to speak to a few interested listeners. Soon a crowd

assembled, some of whom created much noise and commotion. Constables intervened, arrested the two men and conveyed them to Newgate Gaol. At their trial Penn pleaded "Not guilty" and referred the Court to Common Law, quoting many ancient statutes back to Magna Carta. He refused to accept the legality of the indictment. Much indignation was evidenced by the Recorder and his officials, the two prisoners being contemptuously thrust into the bale-dock in the middle of the proceedings. The jury were instructed to consider their verdict regarding both cases. They were unanimous in finding Mead 'Not guilty' and Penn simply 'Guilty of speaking in Gracious Street.' The Recorder refused to accept such a judgment; blustering in his vexation: "You shall bring in another verdict or you shall starve." They were kept for three days and nights without meat or drink, until they should submit; but, stubbornly, this band of men, loyal to right and honour, refused to give anything other than their conscience had decided was just and true. A fine of forty marks apiece still left them unmoved. Three times a verdict of 'Guilty of speaking in Gracious Street' was returned. This was no breaking of any law under the Conventicle Act. Penn's point, therefore, that the indictment was not legal was substantiated. Still infuriated by the attitude of the jury, the Lord Mayor, Sir Samuel Starling, badgered them in every way he could devise, till they were persuaded by their foreman to end the controversy by saying 'Not guilty.' The fines and sentence of imprisonment imposed upon the jurors were quashed by the Court of Common Pleas. Penn and Mead remained in Newgate till their fines were paid for them. Penn had vindicated English

B—P

Common Law with its Trial by Jury; he had placed civil liberty on a firm foundation—a landmark in his struggle for complete religious toleration.

The elder Penn was now very ill and felt the end of his life to be near. With clearer vision than had been his while participating in all the worldly honours which had been bestowed upon him, he saw the righteousness of his son's attitude towards God and man. A complete reconciliation was established between the two. Loe had ended his earthly course in 1668, rejoicing in the certainty of fuller life awaiting him. But for Penn came a further term of imprisonment for refusing to swear an oath at the instigation of the Lord-Lieutenant of the Tower, who was seeking an opportunity to show his intense dislike of the growing spirit of individualism. In the noisome atmosphere of Newgate, amid the felons and vagabonds of the common gaol, full of dirt, disease and death, he wrote *The Great Cause of Liberty of Conscience*. Six months of such dreadful conditions filled him with a great desire to associate with men in Germany and Holland who were moved by the same spirit and seeking for Truth in the same way as himself. Much controversy was rife in England, and Penn was soon busily engaged in all manner of disputations, debatings and writings concerning opinions both without and within his own Society.

In 1672 William Penn married Gulielma Maria Springett, who was eminently fitted for such a partner. Her mother was a seeker and had reached the same conclusions as Penn. Widowed early in life, she had remarried when Gulielma was ten. The child's step-father was the well-known Isaac Pennington, a most ardent Friend, whose home was used as a centre of

Quaker activity, Thomas Ellwood (Milton's secretary) being already established in the household. The little girl grew up in this atmosphere, her whole being permeated with their views and influence. With this bride Penn settled in Rickmansworth[1] for five years of happy home life.

[1] Called Rickmersworth in Penn's letters.

Chapter II

THE GRANTING OF THE CHARTER

GEORGE Fox landed in Bristol in 1673, afire with
zeal and fervour for the cause of the Colonies he had
visited in America, and filled with the spirit of praise
for his miraculous deliverance from every possible
danger. Penn and his wife, who met him, must have
shared his enthusiasm as they listened to his account of
New England, Long Island and East Jersey, and to his
cherished dream of creating in the New World a land
of freedom for the persecuted of the Old. As early as
1631 the Swedes laid out a town called Christina or
Christeen—their first settlement. In 1632 Caecilius
Calvert, Lord Baltimore, obtained from Charles I a
grant of the unoccupied part of Virginia[1]. . . which
the King himself named Maryland in honour of the
Queen, Henrietta Maria. John Printz, the Swedish
Governor, made a treaty with the Indians in 1651, the
latter having complained that the Swedes had introduced much evil among them. In 1659 Lord Baltimore
claimed all the land between 38° and 40° of latitude
from sea to sea. The Dutch, having settled in 1651
and compelled the Swedes to deliver up their forts, sent
out another ship in 1663, and thus, till 1664, New

[1] For fuller account see Robert Proud's *History of Pennsylvania*, of which
these notes are a brief summary.

Sweden and New Netherland continued in their possession. King Charles II, having no great regard for the Dutch, granted on March 20th, 1664, a patent to his brother James, Duke of York and Albany, for sundry tracts of land in America, including New Netherland. The Dutch, being unprepared, were obliged to surrender the country, and their town of New Amsterdam was thenceforward called New York. New Netherland was subsequently divided into New Jersey and New York, the former being granted by James to Lord Berkeley and Sir George Carteret, a Jersey man. In 1675 Lord Berkeley sold his half of the province of New Jersey to a certain John Fenwick in trust for Edward Byllinge. Fenwick was "a litigious old Cromwellian soldier,"[1] recently converted to Quakerism. He sailed in 1675 and landed at a spot which for the "delightsomeness of the land he called Salem."[2] Byllinge, being reduced in circumstances, had agreed to present his interest to his creditors, and William Penn, though, it is said, with reluctance, became joint trustee with two others . . . for the management thereof."[3] In 1676 a deed for five signatories was drawn up as between Sir George Carteret, already established in the eastern half of the province, and the four new Proprietors of the west: Edward Byllinge, William Penn, Gawen Laurie and Nicholas Lucas. The three last-named wrote an epistle of caution to their friends, in which Penn declares that "the Glory and Honor, Power and Wisdom, Truth

[1] A. M. Gummere. "The Settlement of the Jerseys" in R. M. Jones' *Quakers in the American Colonies*. London, 1911 (p. 363).
[2] Ib. p. 366.
[3] In the dispute between Fenwick and Byllinge, Penn, as arbitrator, had recognised the claims of the latter.

and Kingdom of Almighty God is dearer to us than all visible things"; that "our eye hath been single and our hearts sincere." Thousands of emigrants poured into this territory, many of whom were Quakers. In 1679 Sir George Carteret died, and East New Jersey was taken over by twelve proprietors, amongst whom was William Penn. The Jersey Settlements prospered till in 1701 the government was placed quite satisfactorily at the disposal of Queen Anne.

Meanwhile Penn and his confederates were following with keen interest and some anxiety the difficulties with which their fellow-seekers were surrounded, not only in England, but in Holland and Germany. Persecution was rampant—"the foulness of the dungeons into which they were cast, the cruelties of jailers, the impoverishment of families produced untold sufferings, but cemented the Society in a strong family feeling. They volunteered to serve out each other's sentences in jail. 'We do offer up our bodies and selves to you for to put us as lambs into the same dungeons and houses of correction and their straw and nasty holes and prisons, and do stand ready a sacrifice for to go into their places that they may go forth and not die in prison as many of the brethren are dead already.' "[1] "Widows have lost their cows, orphans their beds, labourers their tools," cried Penn indignantly.[2] Curtis, writing to Fox, related how "our little children kept the meetings up when we were all in prison, notwithstanding their wicked Justice when he came and found them there, would pull them out of the meeting and punch

[1] Quoted from Masson's "Life of John Milton and History of the Time," VI, in *A Quaker Experiment in Government*, by Isaac Sharpless. Philadelphia, 1898 (p. 18).

[2] Dobrée. Op. cit., p. 115.

them in the back."[1] "Thomas Curtis and his wife
Anne were the leaders of the Society in Reading—a
society whose sufferings and bravery are outstanding
even in the annals of primitive Quakerism, whose every
convert was a potential martyr."[2] Penn's activities
were ceaseless, both in the field of politics and the
great cause of those suffering from religious tyrannies.
Together with two friends, he made a compilation of
all the cruelties and injustices imposed. Terrible
wrongs needed correction. As many as 4,000 Quakers
were at one time in jail; 243 had died under the
conditions and restrictions of prison life. This was
brought to the notice of the King and Parliament, with
an appeal for the liberty of the victims who, practically
to a man averred (as had Penn himself): "My prison
shall be my grave before I will budge a jot, for I owe
obedience of my conscience to no mortal man."[3] Truly
was this noble heart full of yearning to find a way of
escape for persecuted humanity, more especially those
of his own persuasion. He longed to share and lift
their burdens, as later he was to prove by pleading
with politicians against their sentences; in two cases
when he failed to obtain their acquittal he supported
them in the hour of their martyrdom by being present
at the executions.[4]

Penn's dream of a place of refuge for all who desired
freedom of thought, was to materialise by a marvellous
providing of conditions. Charles II had borrowed

---

[1] Swarthmoor MSS., III, 88. M. R. Brailsford. *The Making of William Penn.* 1930 (p. 238).
[2] Ib., pp. 235-6.   [3] Sharpless. Op. cit., p. 19.
[4] Elizabeth Gaunt burnt by Jefferies for sheltering a political rebel;
Alderman Henry Cornish hanged for alleged conspiracy in the Rye
House Plot.

large sums of money from Admiral Penn, at whose death they became due to his son. The King's extravagance made cash payment improbable; the debt continued to accumulate for several years, growing in amount, but showing no visible sign of settlement. William Penn, with great insight, realised in this state of affairs an opportunity of requesting a grant of land in lieu of money. By 1680 he was owed £16,000, and for this sum he petitioned letters patent for a grant of unoccupied crown territory in America to the north of Maryland. Certain lands there had been apportioned to the Duke of York, who had promised Admiral Penn to befriend his son. Not only did Penn receive the gift of land he desired from Charles, but York also added Delaware. The next thing to be done was to get a Charter drawn up for its government. Lord Baltimore and the Bishop of London presented many demands, with debatable issues, regarding territorial and religious rights to be exercised. The Committee for Trade and Plantations within the Privy Council was satisfied with the terms only after lengthy consideration.[1] On March 14th, 1681, the deed received the royal signature. Penn wished to name his new estate Sylvania, but Charles decided to add Penn to the title—and thus

[1] "The Right Hon'ble the Lords of the Committee for trade and foreign plantations . . . pursuant to His Majesty's Order in Council of the 31st May, 1683, examined the matters between Lord Baltimore and William Penn, Esq., on behalf of His present Majesty concerning a tract of land in America commonly called Delaware. They recommended a division of the land between the Bays of Delaware and Chesapeake into equal parts, one remaining a Crown possession and the other included in Baltimore's territory. To which (and other) propositions the proprietaries of each province signified their consent before the Committee, and declared their readiness to carry the same into execution." This document was dated 13th day of November, 1685, at the Court of Whitehall. It appears in Samuel Hazard's *Register of Pennsylvania*. Oct. 25th, 1828, vol. ii, p. 228.

'Pennsylvania' was his choice because of its suitability
(Penn meaning high or head)[1] and because of his
desire to honour his greatly-loved friend, the late
admiral. Penn was created Proprietary, with complete
possession of the land, subject only to the allegiance
of the inhabitants to the English Crown. He might
make his own laws within the territory, always provided
they were acceptable to English authority. Militarism,
with its display of power and glory was once again to
tempt the man whose soul cried out for love and peace
with all humanity: the Charter included a clause,
presuming to be a protection for him against invasion
and piracy (actually it proved to be a diplomatic way
of securing English control)—he was made a "captain-
general" and invested with power "to levy, muster, and
train all sorts of men."

The attainment of such a Charter without, of course,
the military provisions, had been a dream to him for
many years. At Oxford, twenty years previously, he
had "had an opening of joy to these parts."[2] In April
1681, he wrote: "For the matters of liberty and privilege
I purpose that which is extraordinary, and leave *myself
and succession no power of doing mischief*, that *the will of one
man may not hinder the good of a whole country*."[3] The will
of God was his guide and inspiration in all things. He

[1] Penn once told the Rev. Hugh David that he was himself of Welsh
origin and descended from the Tudors. "My great-grandfather, John
Tudor, lived upon the top of a hill or mountain in Wales and was
generally called John Penmunith, which in English is John-on-the-
Hilltop." . . . His Welsh nickname became abbreviated to John Penn.
J. F. Watson. *Annals of Philadelphia*. Philadelphia, 1844-79 (vol. i, p.
119).
[2] Quoted by Stoughton. Op. cit., p. 165 from Clarkson's *Memoirs of
the Private and Public Life of William Penn*. London, 1849 (vol. i, p. 288).
[3] Letter to Friends. Quoted in full by Janney. Op. cit., p. 172 from
MS. in the *Archives* of American Philosophical Society, Philadelphia.

"eyed the Lord in the obtaining of it" and declared "more was I drawn inward to look to Him and to owe it to His Hand and Power than to any other way I have so obtained it."[1] "It is a clear and just thing, and my God that has given it to me through many difficulties, will, I believe, bless and make it the seed of a nation," he wrote to a friend.[2] With high hope and faith in his ideal he worked out his Frame of Government.[3]

[1] Violet Oakley. *The Holy Experiment*. Philadelphia, 1922.
[2] Stoughton. Op. cit., p. 170.
[3] A recent thesis by Fulmer Mood concerning the granting of the Charter suggests that Penn carefully refrained from admitting any political or religious motive in accepting land from his monarch. But at least one of his biographers (John Stoughton, p. 166) records that the fragments of Penn's petition which were consulted in 1735 "prays that His Majesty, in his compassion to the afflicted, would grant land," etc. This would seem to indicate that Penn freely expressed his "desire to lead multitudes from prison and take them to a land of perfect freedom" (Oakley, op. cit., p. 10). Mood further infers that Charles was only too ready to grant the Charter, in view of existing political conditions in England. The liberty which "Tories could not stomach in their own country might find a home beyond the seas, and a Whig policy be established in security across the ocean." (*Journal* of the Friends' Historical Society, 1935, vol. xxxii).

Chapter III

THE FRAME OF GOVERNMENT

EDMUND BURKE, in his account of European settlements in America, writes that Penn "made the most perfect freedom, both religious and civil, the basis of his establishment; and this has done more towards the settling of the province and towards the settling of it in a strong and permanent manner, than the wisest regulations would have done on any other plan." It was to prove "the model of later American constitutions and the basis of the great Federal Constitution of 1776. . . . The whole code with its reverence for humanity as such was the expression of Quakerism in government."[1]

The Frame was a masterpiece of governmental structure: to Penn government seemed "a part of religion itself, a thing sacred in its institution and end."[2] With such a foundation he considered that it could not be other than a substantial, righteous, and acceptable constitution. George Fox, who had had much experience in the disciplinary framework of the Quaker Society, was an invaluable helper. His ideas had been absorbed by the eager and admiring young disciple for many years, and now the two were ready to set out a plan of action dear to both. It has been suggested

[1] John William Graham. *William Penn.* London, 1916 (pp. 137, 142).
[2] Preface to *The Frame of Government.*

that Sir Algernon Sidney[1] gave Penn the benefit of his
political insight obtained by activities at home and
abroad. In 1679 the latter had used all his powers in
favour of Sir Algernon's return to Parliament. A
majority was won, but the authorities refused to accept
the candidate, who was deemed unsatisfactory. Penn
was greatly disturbed by this, to him, shameful procedure. He felt it to be entirely unjust and regarded
Sir Algernon as hero and martyr, suffering for the
cause of righteousness, a man who was seeking the
highest, regardless of personal well-being. Later he
again rendered Sidney assistance in an election cam-
paign. This time he was returned for Bramber, a little
constituency near Penn's home at Worminghurst, in
Sussex. This politician evidently satisfied Penn's ideal
for an English member of Parliament, who, as he wrote
at the time, "should be able, learned, well-affected to
liberty . . . a respecter of principles but not of
persons."[2] These three great men of their day supple-
mented each other in the development of their well-

[1] Algernon Sidney, the second son of Robert, second Earl of Leicester,
was a man of great ability, who had gained considerable experience in
Denmark, Paris, Rome, and Ireland, before taking up Parliamentary
work in England. After a varied and adventurous career he was involved
in the Monmouth Rebellion and the Rye House Plot, and was beheaded
on a charge of high treason in December 1683.

In a letter to Sidney, dated October 13th, 1681, Penn refers to "the
discourse we had together at my house, about my drawing constitutions
not as proposals but as fixt to the hand," continuing, "and also that
I took my pen, and immediately I drew the termes, so as they corre-
sponded (and truly, I thought, more properly) with thy objection and
sense. Upon this thou didst draw a draught as to the frame of government, gave it to me to read, and we discourst it with a considerable
argument; it was afterwards called for back by thee to finish and polish
and I suspended proceeding in the business of government ever since."
Letter from William Penn to Algernon Sidney, reprinted in Hazard's
Register, vol. xiv, p. 223, from *Memoirs* of the Pennsylvania Historical
Society.

[2] Dixon. Op. cit., p. 170.

balanced scheme; George Fox supplied what Sidney lacked, "faith in things unseen and passionate belief in individual men."[1]   Penn had vision; Fox knew the power of the Spirit; Sidney was zealous for an uprightness in governments, in contrast to the methods practised at that time.   Together they incorporated into their Frame of Government the following principles:

1. Democracy, as men then understood it.

2. Complete religious liberty.

3. Justice and fairness in dealing with aborigines and neighbours.

4. The absence of all military and naval provision for attack and defense.

5. The abolition of oaths.[2]

---

[1] Ib., p. 55.

[2] See Sharpless, op. cit., pp. 1-3. In vol. i of the *Collection of the Works of William Penn*, London, 1726, there is a "Treatise on Oaths" (p. 614). Ten reasons are given why the early Friends considered that to take an oath was both unreasonable and, from a moral and spiritual standpoint, undesirable. The first declares that: "Diseased Men only want Remedies, and Lame Men Crutches. Honesty needs neither Whip nor Spur . . . and Men of Virtue will speak truth without Extortings. For Oaths are a sort of Racks to the Mind, altogether useless where integrity sways. . . . How is it possible for Men to recover their ancient Confidence, that good men reposed in one another if some don't lead the way? (ib., p. 615). The second says: "We dare not swear because we dare not lie" (ib., p. 615) and in paragraph v Penn asks: "What need is there of that Man's being awed into true Evidence by such sort of Attestations and Imprecations as make up the common form of oaths, who knows God to be always present to reside and preside in his Soul?" (ib., pp. 616-617). This confession of faith in the Inward Light is followed by a witness of the immanence and omnipresence of the Creator. Paragraph vii states that: "We look upon it to be not less than a presumptuous tempting of God to summon Him as Witness not only to our Terence, but trivial businesses. Besides it is vain and insolent to think, that a Man when he pleaseth, can make the *Great God of Heaven* a Witness or Judge in any Matter to appear by some signal Approbation or Judgment, to help or forsake him, as the Truth or Falsness of his Oath requires when he saith, *So help me God*" (ib., p. 617).

Most of these ideas had been mooted at some time in history, but never had the whole collection been tried. How these principles succeeded and their influence persisted in the minds of men, is shown unquestionably in the statement of Maître André Philippe, Counsel for Defence in the trial of Philippe Vernier, in France in 1933, on a charge of conscientious objection to conscription for military training. He said: "finally the community of Quakers who created the first *State without an army*, that of Pennsylvania, during the last war, while refusing to do murder, were able to win the sympathy of all by their work of international relief."[1]

The Frame was composed of 24 Articles and 40 Laws:[2] temporary proposals, approved by English authority, and subject to alteration and development as the appointed Council and Assembly should find conditions necessitate. The Articles appointed an administration, which was to establish a code of statutes based on the aforesaid laws. This Administration was to consist of a Provincial Council and a General Assembly, the former to be presided over by the Proprietor (or his Deputy) and the members to be chosen by universal manhood suffrage. Its numbers were to remain constant—72 at first elected, 24 retiring at the end of each year, 24 others filling their places. The Council was to concern itself with the welfare of the State; its finance, its laws, and safety; the provision of new towns, ports, schools and roads; and the en-

---

[1] *The Trial of Philippe Vernier*. Abbreviated translation from the *Cahiers de la Réconciliation*, published by Henry Roser. Translated by Helen Carpenter. Friends' Peace Committee, 1933.

[2] Would Pennsylvania have been better without any formulated legal code, in view of the difficulties with regard to the 'penal sanctions' subsequently employed to enforce it?

couragement of scientific inventions which would serve many useful and progressive purposes. The General Assembly was at first to comprise all the freemen of the province; later not more than 200 were to be elected by ballot. These men had no constructional rights: they might not initiate or propose bills; their business was to amend, reject or accept measures brought forward by the Council. The 40 provisional laws related mainly to religious liberty, civil justice, and amelioration of conditions for prisoners, the poor, orphans, and needy in any respect; to be decided on as occasions arose, for Penn, with Sidney, realised that "no men can know what laws are needful so well as those whose lives, properties, and liberties are concerned."[1] Criminals were to be tried by jury; county court cases were to be treated by "three peace-makers or arbitrators," in order to spare the ordeal of expensive and prolonged litigation. Fees were limited and publicly exhibited. Prisons were to be houses where confinement was alleviated by work;[2] men were to be regarded always as men with a personality to which reverence is due.[3] In England prisoners were thrust into veritable hells

[1] W. Hepworth Dixon. Op. cit., p. 194.

[2] Thomas Clarkson in his *Memoirs of the Public and Private Life of William Penn* (written in 1849) states: "At the present day in Pennsylvania . . . no corporal punishment is allowed in the prison. A hope is held out to the prisoners that the time of their confinement may be shortened by their good behaviour. . . . In consequence of these regulations (those of a free workshop) great advantages have arisen both to the criminals and to the State. The State, it is said, has experienced a diminution of crimes to the amount of one half since this change in the penal system . . . built upon the Christian principle of the reformation of the offender. This system *obtains nowhere but in Pennsylvania,* and it is *the direct germ,* only trained up by other hands, of the root that was planted in the constitution of that country by William Penn" (pp. 346-7).

[3] See Appendix I.

for quite minor transgressions; a truly revolting state
of indifference or cruelty was shown to them. At least
200 offences were punishable by death. Penn, with one
great gesture, made these things impossible in Pennsylvania. He confined the death penalty to murder or
treason. He instituted an entirely new penal system,
whereby the prisoner was allowed to keep his self-
respect and was helped to reform his character. The
prevention of crime was pre-eminent in the mind of
this great lover of humanity. He formed special courts
where orphan cases should be investigated with the idea
of making proper provision for them; all children were
to be given a good education, and every one, rich or
poor, was to be trained to some kind of trade or
profession, "all work being honourable in a democratic
state, all idleness a shame."[1] He worked with an
urgency of spirit, to the end that all children should
grow up to be men and women who believed in
Almighty God and desired to live in peace and friendli-
ness with each other, untrammelled in conscience, free
in mind, and well equipped physically to face the
conditions of the world. This would be the embodiment
of the *Holy Experiment* which he had envisaged for
years: an example to all nations of a way of living at
peace with all men.

[1] Dixon. Op. cit., p. 212.

Chapter IV

PENNSYLVANIA

"New forest-homes beyond the mighty sea,
There undisturbed and free
To live as brothers of one family."[1]

THE Frame of Government for Pennsylvania was enacted and signed in England by the Governor and freemen in 1682. Certain lands in Delaware were added by the Duke of York. For these Penn obtained deeds of conveyance for the satisfaction of the people already living there. He set to work at once making elaborate preparations for leaving England (as if for ever), and starting to colonise the American territory. A Free Society of Traders[2] had been established in Bristol, whose members had unusual privileges and worked in striking co-operation—for, whilst sharing the benefits of communal trading, they preserved the rights of the individual to trade personally, but no monopolies were to be granted. This company was used by Penn to set up a line of commerce between England and Pennsylvania. His project was made known generally: detailed arrangements for the well-being of his family were planned. His cousin, Captain William Markham,

[1] Whittier's Translation of the Latin of Francis Daniel Pastorius in the Germantown Records, 1688.
[2] See Appendix II.

who had been sent out some months previously, had prepared the way for his coming; commissioners had been instructed to arrange for a settlement, lay out a town[1] and negotiate with the people concerning the occupation of lands. Everything being ready for his departure, he chartered the *Welcome* to sail from Deal on September 1st, 1682. About 100 Quakers accompanied him. It was autumn, and the prospects of a pleasant voyage not too bright. Unfortunately, too, smallpox broke out; as many as thirty cases proved fatal and terror seized the remaining passengers. Panic was averted by the conduct of Penn, who nursed the sick, comforted the afflicted, fed the poor from his own table, and endeavoured to inspirit them and keep alive their faith in God. "The good conversation of William Penn was very advantageous to all the company."[2] Two months were spent at sea, the *Welcome*'s passengers getting more and more anxious and eager for sight of land. On October 24th, 1682, they arrived at New Castle, Delaware, where people representing all the nations in Pennsylvania gathered to greet the new Governor. Next day he presented his "deeds of enfeoffment, and John Moll, Esq., and Ephraim Hannan, gentlemen, performed livery of seisin by handing over to him turf and twig, water and soil."[3] So did Penn become possessor of this territory—land of his dreams, now realised!

[1] Among the instructions which Penn issued to the commissioners who had been appointed to "settle a great town" was the following: "Let every house be placed in the middle of its platt, as to the breadth way of it, that so there may be ground on each side of it for gardens, or orchards, or fields, that it may be a green country town which will never be burnt and always be wholesome." Hazard's *Register*, vol. x, p. 92.

[2] Janney. Op. cit., p. 205.　　　　[3] Stoughton. Op. cit., p. 183.

He began at once to visit various localities, calling upon the Duke in New York, and later proceeding to East Jersey. The Council meanwhile was considering its position and the new Constitution. Early in December *the Right Honourable Proprietary* held a court. *The Great Law* (or body of laws of the Province) was accepted, but alterations were proposed for the numbers and powers of the Council and Assembly. The Assembly demanded certain additional powers for itself: a new Charter was drafted and submitted to Penn in March 1683. His treble vote was annulled and the Assembly claimed the right to introduce Bills; Thomas Wynne was to replace Nicholas Moore as Speaker, and a code of representation was drawn up to meet the requirements of members. The Right Honourable Proprietary cheerfully gave way in the matter of his own vote; he remained true to his principle of freedom in the State; but he could not yield the power which belonged to him and the Council to make laws—his plan for safeguarding the Constitution.

The founding of a capital city was the next concern. It was to be a green city in a green land, with gardens and trees, open spaces and well-built homesteads. The pleasant spot approved by Penn lay bounded by two mighty arms of a river, stately woods banking their sides, a truly sylvan gem, worthy of the noble township shortly to grace the new colony and stand as testimony to the love of beauty, peace and freedom which was in very deed part of the man who was giving his whole heart to the outworking of his ideal. A few scattered houses were in sight with all the signs of country life around, and a foundation was laid upon which was reared Philadelphia, that is to say, the city of brotherly love.

This Minute of a Friends' Meeting is recorded treating of his arrival: "At a monthly meeting the 8th of 9th month (November), 1682. At this time Governor Penn and a multitude of Friends arrived here and erected a city called Philadelphia, about half a mile from Shackamaxon, where meetings were established."[1]

The city grew prosperously, everyone sharing in the work earnestly and zealously. In a few months as many as 80 houses were ready; two years later 600 had been built; another year saw the opening of a small school, to be followed in six years (1689) by the famous centre of scholarship, known subsequently as the William Penn Charter School. Within the first few years of its existence Philadelphia had a postal system [2] and a printing press.

The focal point of Pennsylvania was thus laid out ready to attract emigrants. "I went thither to lay the foundation of a free colony for all mankind that should go thither, more especially those of my own profession," Penn wrote to Roger Mompesson—and well indeed he succeeded, for emigrants poured in from all quarters, England, Ireland, Holland and Germany. Among the latter was Francis Daniel Pastorius, whose life and ministry form the theme of Whittier's poem, "The Pennsylvanian Pilgrim." He came as a Mennonite, rejoicing in this glorious opportunity of living in the

[1] Watson's *Annals*, I, 132. Quoted by Janney. Op. cit., p. 208. For account of Penn's Treaty with the Indians at Shackamaxon see Chapter V.

[2] In 1683 William Penn established a Post Office and appointed Henry Waldy of Sachony, Post-master. He fixed the rates of postage thus: Letters from the Falls (of the Delaware) to Philadelphia, 3d.; to Chester, 6d.; to New Castle, 7d.; to Maryland, 6d. The post went once a week, and its movements were regularly published on the meeting-house door, and other public places (Hazard's *Register*, vol. x, p. 92).

way he desired. He laid out Germantown in 1685 to be the Philadelphia of German colonists. Very soon his conscience was touched to see the evil of slavery among the peoples, and he was the first to bring his "concern" against the holding of negroes in bondage before his own Meeting. This was in 1688.

The question of witchcraft in a community is often a considerable danger to its progress, its sense of security and well-being. In 1683 two Swedes (a man and a woman) were brought before the Court accused of sorcery. Some of the inhabitants of Chester, formerly the Swedish settlement of Upland, believed that they had "boiled the flesh of a calf which, as everyone knew, had died of a spell."[1] The case was decided by a jury, who, according to Penn's masterly way of dealing with the woman, gave a verdict of being famed a witch, but not guilty of the particular accusation brought against her. This powerful and tactful attitude of the Governor quite effectively uprooted the trouble. No further cases were known in Pennsylvania.

The Pennsylvanian Quakers "had a testimony" against law-courts[2] in spite of the justice and fairness of trials. Many grievances naturally arose, such as a man buying land when advised not to do so by Friends; the ruins of a miller's dam were destroyed; a stream of water was turned back into its natural course; many individual and personal offences were perpetrated. These, however, were dealt with, as amicably and generously as possible in their Monthly Meetings, and disciplinary measures were imposed. Usually therefore the cases were settled without recourse to litigation.

[1] Dobrée. Op. cit., p. 214.
[2] Sharpless. Op. cit., p. 23.

Despite Penn's efforts to get all disputes peaceably settled in his own affairs as well as those of the people, he had one long struggle with Lord Baltimore on a question of boundaries. An error of judgment in determining latitudes had resulted in assigning territory to Maryland which should have belonged to Delaware. Penn would have been thus deprived of almost invaluable property (sea-ports commanding the bay), which made it necessary for him to substantiate his claim. He approached Lord Baltimore with a genuine desire to rectify the mistake, and to show him how futile was his attempt to demand right of possession. "The mildness of his measures and the courtesy of his defence, stand out in bold relief when contrasted with the proceedings of his antagonist." [1] All sorts of annoyances became real sources of anxiety when armed men were posted in a fort within a few miles of New Castle with intention to destroy the town. So virulent were Baltimore's measures and so involved the dispute, that it had to be taken to England to be decided by the Lords of the Committee of Trade and Plantations.

At this time, too, rumours of persecutions in England of the most unjust and atrocious nature reached Penn's ever-open ear, and touched to the quick his noble heart. Men were being "seized . . . and hurried off to . . . gaol" [2] by soldiers for no further offence than meeting together for worship. Hundreds were filling the noisome prisons for their religious beliefs and practices, many dying under the foul conditions and penalties inflicted. Penn was living here in Pennsylvania, where freedom was the order of the day; in

[1] Janney. Op. cit., p. 253.
[2] Stoughton. Op. cit., p. 200.

a land which had enabled him to realise much of his life-long aspiration; in a lovely home, Pennsbury Manor, prepared by William Markham, laid out amid groves of poplars and flower gardens, trees having been sent from England to beautify the "mansion-house" of this benefactor of mankind. He could not bear to stay here longer while his fellow-Friends were suffering under such contrasting circumstances. As the boundary decision would most assuredly call for his presence in England, he determined to leave Philadelphia and return home. He embarked on the *Endeavour* in August 1684, leaving Thomas Lloyd as President of the Council.

In a letter written to the Society of Traders Penn thus speaks of the land of his adoption: "The country itself, its soil, air, water, seasons, and produce, both natural and artificial, are not to be despised. . . . The air is sweet and clear, and the heavens serene, like the south part of France . . . the waters are generally good . . . the woods are adorned with lovely flowers for colour, greatness, figure, and variety. . . . I bless God I am fully satisfied with the country and entertainment I got in it."[1] On another occasion he writes: "Oh, how sweet is the quiet of these parts, free from the anxious and troublesome solicitations, hurries, and perplexities of woeful Europe."[2]

His appreciation of the colony with its opportunities for pure and true religious living, led him to exhort the settlers he was leaving behind to "Have a care of cumber, and the love and care of the world . . . have a care of looseness, for it becometh us to be watchful

[1] Janney. Op. cit., pp. 239, 248.
[2] Stoughton. Op. cit., p. 193.

. . . have a care of naturalness in the profession of the truth . . . love one another, and help and assist and comfort one another . . . have a care of a perverse spirit . . . then your tents shall be goodly and your dwellings glorious." [1]

Such was the democracy instituted by Penn in the New World—the "Government an executive dependent for its support on the people; all subordinate elective officers elected by the people; the judiciary dependent for its existence on the people; all legislation originating exclusively with the people; no forts, no armed force . . . no militia, no established church, no difference of rank and a harbor open for the reception of all mankind of every nation, of children of every language and every creed." [2]   *Would such a seeming Utopia live through the ages?*

[1] Janney. Op. cit., pp. 255-6.
[2] Bancroft. *History of the United States.* Quoted by Sharpless. Op. cit., p. 67.

Chapter V

THE INDIANS

"THE Iroquois alliance with the English forms the chief fact in American history down to 1763," according to Lewis H. Morgan.[1] Three great divisions of aborigines occupied the basin of the St. Lawrence in the seventeenth century—Algonquins, Hurons, and Iroquois. Of these the latter were of far the greatest political importance, the family occupying three territories, North, South and South-east; wherein prosperous grain-growing villages were inhabited by a people, sincere and simple in their religious ritual and practices, but utterly ruthless in time of warfare, making a palisaded stronghold of their own district from which to sally forth upon the enemy. In 1570 five tribes joined together for strength and safety in a Great Federation celebrated in history as the *Five Nations:* Mohawk, Oneida, Onondaga, Cayuga, Seneca. (The Tuscaroras joined them in 1715, making the Six Nations of the Long House.[2]) The Confederation

---

[1] Quoted from *Encyclopædia Britannica* (Eleventh Edition), article on "Indians, North American," p. 475.

[2] This term is thus explained by Henry R. Schoolcraft in his *Notes on the Iroquois*, Albany, 1847 (p. 48): "Each tribe had, at some period of their progress, a distinctive appellation, as Onondaya, Oneida, etc. . . . When they came to confederate, and form a general council, they took the name of Konoshioni (or, as the French authors write it, Acquino-

occupied the State of New York; each tribe managed its own affairs under a *sachem*, a council of fifty, meeting annually. They maintained friendly relations with the Dutch and English settlers, but bitter hostility was evinced against the French. An alliance between some of their tribes and the Dutch resulted in their obtaining arms. With guns in their possession they could, and did, succeed in conquering almost all their neighbours in the seventeenth century, and intimidated the Delawares throughout a long period—till finally, in 1720, they submitted.

The Hurons were occupying the lands round and about Ontario. White men strayed into this territory; solitary hunters went into the fields and forests to kill, and often slew an Indian who chanced to be in his path. Free trappers wandered at will and often exterminated the natives of whole districts. French fur companies came into existence, which, while taking the Indian's property, took care to preserve him for purposes of trade.

Adjoining this region was the home of the Algonquins, who gradually absorbed further possessions from James River, in Virginia, coastwards and westwards to the Rocky Mountains, finally surrounding Hurons and Iroquois. Early in the seventeenth century French fur-traders established themselves in Quebec, originally founded by Samuel Champlain, who very soon decided to help his Algonquian neighbours against their

shioni) meaning, literally, People of the Long House, and figuratively, a United People, a term by which they still denominate themselves when speaking in a national sense. . . . This Long House, to employ their own figure, extended east and west from the present site of Albany to the foot of the great lakes, a distance by modern admeasurement of 325 miles.

Iroquian enemies. An alliance was entered upon which had much to do with the final defeat of the French in North America. The battle fought and won by Champlain near Ticonderoga in 1609, made the Iroquois the lasting antagonists of the French, and since the former held a large portion of what is now the State of New York, the latter were effectually prevented from annihilating the English colonies to the south. Nevertheless, Frontenac, Governor of New France (Canada), continually planned attacks upon New England, encouraging ruthless border warfare and making merciless raids upon the Iroquois. The latter grew embittered against the French and decided to ally themselves with the English, whose numbers were so very much greater, twenty to one; this added strength enabled them to keep France entirely cut off from Lake Ontario, her access to western territory, and also cut off her boundaries southwards, because of the Iroquois peoples. Had this state of affairs not been maintained, the English colonies would have been flanked by the French instead of the natives, and the history of North America might have been an entirely different story.

While Frontenac was vainly endeavouring to force the Five Nations to submit to his 'power and protection'[1] missionaries of the Jesuit Order were trying to win them through religion. They were no more successful in this than in the former attempt at coercion. A few Indians were 'converted' and segregated, but no hold could be obtained which would further French political interests —the Iroquois were only exasperated to more and more bitter resentment. Efforts to gain the favour or obedi-

[1] J. A. Doyle. *The Middle Colonies.* 1907. p. 289.

ence of these peoples were entirely fruitless, except a few individual converts to Jesuitism.

These same peoples had shown a very different spirit towards those who came to them as messengers of the Friends' Society. As early as 1658 "Josiah Coale and Thomas Thurston were treated with the utmost kindness by the Indians in the course of their dangerous overland journey from Virginia to New York. A little later, in New England, after Josiah Coale and John Copeland had been beaten and imprisoned by the white settlers, the former found a safe refuge among the Indians. So it was that the natives received the blessing of the early Quaker apostles who, footsore, sick and afflicted, found rest in the wigwams, and comfort in the humble ministrations of the children of the forest."[1]

"When William Penn petitioned Charles II for a grant of land in America, he stated that one of his objects was the conversion of the poor Indians to Christ's Kingdom 'by just and upright measures.' He foresaw that the *practice* of the Christian virtues would be more convincing than the preaching of them. . . . The *practice* of the Christian virtues in dealing with the Indians was a very passion among Friends."[2] Charles II was not at all sure that such 'measures' would be powerfully protective enough for this young enthusiast; he felt he must add some means of safeguarding both men and territories; he exclaimed to Penn: "Why, man, what security have you that you will not be in their war-kettle in two hours after setting foot on their

---

[1] Rayner Wickersham Kelsey. *Friends and the Indians*. Philadelphia, 1917 (p. 42).
[2] Kelsey. Op. cit., p. 40.

shore?"[1] Hence the provision was interpolated in the Charter of the right to make war on the Indians, and to pursue them "even without the limits of the said province and by God's assistance to vanquish and take them, and being taken, to put them to death by the law of war, or to save them," at his pleasure. "The conduct of the settlers in the neighbouring colonies did not consist of those *just and gentle manners* which the Pennsylvanian Charter prescribed. The first thing they did was to raise forts, to make a show with their arms, to exercise themselves in the same. . . . They tried rather to outwit than to be just."[2]

Early in 1682 Markham had been instructed by Penn to purchase certain lands for his immediate occupation. After his arrival he spent months surveying and considering before he attempted to procure further properties. This idea of transaction between natives and whites was not a new thing; much earlier in history such dealings had been established on an honourable trading basis by the Dutch, who were careful to ensure full value for land being paid to the Indians. The price Penn offered was in every case satisfactory to the people; though it would seem by modern standards a strange balance, yet it was really just and fair. Presumably the methods used were similar to those of the Quakers in New Jersey: kettles, clothing, lead, looking-glasses, knives, axes, fish-hooks, scissors, red-paint, needles, bells and such-like were some of the articles given in exchange.[3] When he had been offered £6,000

[1] Oakley. Op. cit., *The Holy Experiment*, p. viii.

[2] Clarkson. Op. cit., p. 353.

[3] Such purchases were always secured by deeds which were preserved and recorded.

and 2½ per cent of their profits by a company for a monopoly of trading with the Indians he had definitely rejected the proposal. "I did refuse a great temptation last second day (he confessed in a letter to Robert Turner) . . . but as the Lord gave it to me over all and great opposition I would not abuse His love, nor act unworthy of His providence, and so defile what came to me clean." Furthermore, Penn insisted on all the dealings between his people and the Indians being absolutely and unquestionably just. "In the *'Certain Conditions or Concessions'* agreed upon it was stipulated that whatever was sold to the Indians should be sold *in the public market-place and suffer the test whether good or bad."* [1]

By every means in his power the Governor of Pennsylvania worked to win the friendship and brotherly confidence of his new compatriots. He wrote letters to them; he drew up treaties of amity with at least nineteen different tribes; he laid out several thousand pounds "to instruct, support and oblige them"; he "had occasion to be in council with them upon terms for land. . . . When the purchase was agreed great promises passed between us and good Neighbourhood, and that the Indians and English must live in love so long as the sun and moon give light." [2] As a further preliminary to the Great Pact [3] which followed, Penn made friends with the Indians known as the Lenni Lenapé (Delawares). These were a strange, proud people with a deep sense of religion, "a firm belief in a cosmic mystery present throughout all nature, called *manilou* (or manitou) . . . identified with both animate

---

[1] Clarkson. Op. cit., p. 104.   [2] Kelsey. Op. cit.
[3] The Treaty of Shackamaxon.

and inanimate objects, and the impulse was strong to enter into personal relation with the mystic power."[1] They were of ancient Algonquian stock, and were revered as 'grandfathers' among the three great North American aboriginal races. They were peace-loving and self-developing; before white men appeared they had a most comprehensive system of education—the young being instructed in the whole round of economic pursuits—"handicrafts, agriculture, household work, . . . speech, fine art, customs, etiquette, social obligations and tribal lore."[2] The health of babies and young children was given particular attention, and they were well supplied with toys, playthings, and games. Quite early in life they were initiated into the mysteries of religious and social ideas. Corporal punishment was little in vogue, being "condemned as bad for the soul as well as the body."[3] Parental affection was as highly developed as with whites, and individuality was encouraged and given freedom of growth. Certainly they were no mean branch of a worthy people.

The Shawnee of Pennsylvania also received the solicitous attention of this Quaker politician. "The Six Nations of New York claimed a suzerainty over the Pennsylvanian Indians, and in this capacity, Penn, in 1696, bought of them, or of the Governor of New York, acting for them, the lands on both sides of the Susquehanna throughout the whole province. He explained that he was only buying the right of the Six Nations."[4] Consequently, the Indians of North America accepted Penn as a friend and benefactor. ". . . Because he

[1] See article on "Indians" in *Enc. Brit.*, 11th Edn., p. 472.
[2] Mason. Ib., p. 480.
[3] Ib., p. 480.   [4] Dobrée. Op. cit., p. 181.

never cheated them, never tried to outwit them, and above all because he went about among them as though he were one of themselves, they never betrayed his trust in them." In 1727 the Chief of the Five Nations told the Governor: "Governor Penn, when he came into this province took all the Indians by the hand; he embraced them as his friends and brethren and made a firm league of friendship with them."[1]

This was his method of approach in the Great Treaty of Amity whose date is uncertain, the place of which rests on tradition and whose objects are not positively known. June 23rd, 1683, has been given,[2] but Penn's own letters ascribe it to the autumn of the previous year.[3] Certain it is that Penn lost little time after his arrival in the colonies before arranging an official gathering of the Indians to meet him and his men in friendly discussion of relationships. "On the banks of the Delaware, in the suburbs of the rising city of Philadelphia, lay a natural amphitheatre, used from time immemorial as the place of meeting for the native tribes."[4] A stately elm-tree stood forth as a suitable centre for the ceremony. Taminent (or Tamanend), the chief sachem, acted as the Indian 'king'; behind him, forming a picturesque crescent, sat men, women and children. In orderly and expectant silence they waited for Penn and his colleagues, who were approaching the scene in a barge. As they alighted and moved towards the Indians' fire Taminent rose, put on his chaplet and horn (emblems of kingly authority), and

---

[1] *Colonial Records*, vol. iii, p. 288. Quoted by Sharpless, p. 164.
[2] *Pennsylvania Mag.*, vol. vi, p. 218.
[3] Bowdoin. *History of Friends in America.* Quoted by Doyle. Op. cit., p. 504.
[4] Dixon. Op. cit., p. 286.

greeted his guests in the name of 'the nations' who were ready to hear him. Penn responded in his inimitable, kindly, and gracious manner: "The Great Spirit, who made me and you . . . knows that I and my friends have a hearty desire to live in peace and friendship with you, and to serve you to the utmost of our power. It is not our custom to use hostile weapons against our fellow-creatures, for which reason we have come unarmed. . . . We are met on the broad pathway of good faith and good will, so that no advantage is to be taken on either side, but all to be openness, brotherhood, and love. . . . I will consider you as the same flesh and blood with the Christians and the same as if one's man's body were to be divided into two parts."[1] Gravely the Indians listened; long they deliberated; then one advanced, saluted Penn in the king's name, took him by the hand, and pledged kindness and good neighbourhood, and that the Indians and English must live in love as long as the sun and moon shall endure. These sentiments accorded well with the Englishman's purpose of friendship and equality, as "between all the children of one Divine Father . . . not to lead to any exercise of superior authority."[2] The whole scene was embellished with elaborate details, showing mutual confidence, as evidence of a deep and sincere religious conviction. "They meant no harm and had no fear. He (Penn) laid his scroll on the ground. No oaths, no seals, no mummeries were used; the treaty was ratified on both sides with yea! and was kept."[3] It was "the only league made between those nations and the Christians,

[1] Janney. Op. cit., p. 214   [2] Doyle. Op. cit., p. 504
[3] Dixon. Op. cit., p. 220.

D—p

which was never sworn to by oath, and never violated."[1]
An interpreter conveyed the speeches and each transaction was recorded in writing to be preserved and
made constitutional.   In such dramatic fashion was
made the Pact[2] which "was the foundation of the most
successful treatment of aborigines that history records.
No drop of Quaker blood was shed by an Indian. No
breach of the peace occurred for over seventy years,
till the war party and the church party at home
succeeded in dispossessing the Quaker government of
the colony."[3]

Thirty-five years later (1728) Patrick Gordon met
the Indian tribes associated with Shackamaxon who
approached, free from any sense of fear, the English
Governor of Pennsylvania who was a white man like

---

[1] Voltaire. *Lettres Philosophiques*. Quoted by Dobrée.

[2] Doubts have been expressed from time to time with regard to the
Treaty, and it has even been suggested that as an historical incident it
never actually took place in the way tradition has represented it.
References to the place and date are to be found in Hazard's *Register*,
vol. xv, p. 117, where Redmond Conyngham contributes some historical
notes relating to the votes of the Assembly. He states that Big Beaver
mentioned the Treaty in 1753, and also that the reason why his speech
does not appear in the printed account of the Treaty made at Carlisle,
is explained on p. 528 of the fourth volume of the votes of Assembly,
where it is declared that "it was thought to relate more particularly
to the Proprietary than to the Province."   We are informed that
Teedyuscung referred to the Treaty and that the reason why the
"Minutes of the Indian Conference in relation to the Great Treaty
made with William Penn at the Big Tree, Shackamaxon, on the four-
teenth day of the tenth month, 1682," cannot now be found, may be
explained "because they were thought to relate more particularly to
the Proprietary than to the Province, and therefore were kept among
the private papers of the Proprietary."   Conyngham refers the reader
to Gordon's *History of Pennsylvania*, p. 603, where the same date and
place are given in connection with Penn's meeting with the Indians.
A note explains that 'tenth month' means December, and not October
as "the year formerly commenced with March as the first month."

[3] J. W. Graham. Op. cit., p. 160.

their late beloved *Onas*.[1] He addressed the gathering in the friendly spirit expected of him. He enumerated for their remembrance the main points of the Great Treaty, and having commended the Indians in that they had been faithful to their leagues with the English, had kept their hearts clean, and preserved the chain of affinity from rust, he trusted they would continue in this practice; that all Christians and Indians should be brethren; that paths and houses should be free and open to one another; that neither should hurt the other, nor their creatures; that any mistaken harm done should be speedily rectified and forgotten; that neither Christian nor Indian should believe any false rumours or reports, but should enquire into the truth as brethren together; and, above all, they should each acquaint their children with the league of friendship between them, that it might grow stronger and stronger and be kept clean and bright "while the creeks and rivers run, and while the sun, moon, and stars endure."[2]

It was not without good purpose that Governor Gordon mentioned taking note of 'false reports,' since an alarm had been attempted and had proved abortive. Two Indian women of New Jersey had circulated a story that the Indians were going to surround and cut off all the English, march on Philadelphia and massacre the immigrants. So persistently was this rumour spread that the Council could not afford to ignore it. Caleb Pusey and five other Friends offered their services to

---

[1] It is interesting to note that the familiar terms '*Onas*' and '*Miquon*' were used for Penn by the Iroquois and Delaware Indians respectively, both words signifying a quill or pen. Lenni Lenape means "the original people." The name connected with the doubtful situation of the Great Treaty was Sakimaxing, meaning "the place of kings," later corrupted by white men to Shackamaxon.

[2] Janney. Op. cit., p. 217.

discover the truth of the matter. Unarmed, they proceeded to the scene of the supposed hostile gathering, where they found an old chief surrounded by women and children. Not a young man was present; not a sign of any kind of aggression appeared.[1] Similarly in one of Penn's early reports from the colony (*A Further Account of Pennsylvania*), he alludes to a false report of a massacre by Indians which had been circulated in England. "The dead people were alive at our last advices," he writes, and adds: "Our humanity obliges them so far that they generally leave their guns at home when they come to our settlements. . . . Justice gains and awes them."[2]

There was peace without any sort of conflict in Pennsylvania from 1681 till 1755—despite conditions in neighbouring colonies. In 1704 Thomas Chalkley reports concerning New England that "the Indians were very barbarous in the destruction of the English inhabitants, scalping some and knocking out the brains of others. They (the Indians) told him that they had no quarrel with the Quakers *for they were a quiet, peaceable people and hurt nobody, and that therefore none should hurt them.*"[3] Three Friends who were false to the principles of their way of life met with diaster, because they were regarded as militants. In Massachusetts two men carrying guns and a woman who attempted to take refuge in a garrison were promptly and unceremoniously slain.[4] Without provocation the Indians maintained

[1] Proud. I, p. 337. Quoted by Margaret Hirst, *The Quakers in Peace and War*, p. 368.

[2] *Pennsylvania Magazine*, IX, p. 79.

[3] Clarkson. Op. cit., p. 356.

[4] The source of the oft-told tale of the three Quakers who perished at the hands of the Indians, may be found in a volume entitled *A Collection*

peace, for as a Friend in early days states: "Without any carnal weapon we entered the land and inhabited therein as safe as if there had been thousands of garrisons, for the Most High preserved us from harm, both man and beast."[1]

So long as the Quakers remained true to their profession of faith, so long was this state of amity between Red man and White man.[2] The great spirit of William Penn, lover of humanity and truly devoted to its service, held the people in a common bond of confidence and trust. At his death his wife continued his work, and nothing disturbed this relationship until 1736, when two sons of William (John and Thomas) became Proprietors in Pennsylvania. Regardless of Governor or Council, these two perpetrated a deliberate

---

of the Works of that Ancient and Faithful Servant of Jesus Christ, Thomas Chalkley (London, 1766).

Describing the onslaughts of the Indians in 1704, Chalkley declares that "among the hundreds that were slain, I heard but of three of our Friends being killed, whose destruction was very remarkable, as I was informed the one was a Woman, the other two were Men. The Men used to go to their Labour without any weapons, and trusted to the Almighty, and depended on his Providence to protect them (it being their Principle not to use weapons of War to offend others, or defend themselves), but the spirit of distrust taking place in their minds they took Weapons of War to defend themselves, and the Indians . . . now seeing they have Guns, and supposing they designed to kill the Indians they therefore shot the Men dead" (p. 41).

Then follows the history of the woman who took refuge in a fort, which is told by her daughter, Margaret Doe, who does not hesitate to express her misgivings at her mother's lack of faith, and her own sense of shame at its fatal consequence (pp. 42-45).

[1] Quoted by M. Hirst.

[2] Penn wrote a letter to the Indians (or their chief) under the title of the Emperor of Canada, in which he said: "The people who come with me are a just, plain, and honest people, that neither make war upon others, nor fear war from others because they will be just." The letter goes on to explain the purpose of the Society of Traders which Penn has "set up in my province to traffick with thee and thy people for your Commodities, that you may be furnished with that which is just and good at reasonable rates." Hazard's *Register*, vol. ix, p. 112.

fraud upon the Indians, known afterwards as 'The Walking Purchase,'[1] a source of continual rancour with the natives, and a breakdown of their confidence. The Penns desired to purchase certain land to be measured and assigned by both sides. The Englishmen cheated in the measuring and claimed territory unjustly. The deeds were presented to the Council, which accepted them without inquiry. Later, when Teedy-uscung demanded that they be produced, it was done very reluctantly, giving further cause for annoyance. Disputes between Delawares and Iroquois followed, insults and false charges leading to more and more trouble; the Six Nations laid claim to the Pennsylvanian Indians as their subjects; conferences were held, and eventually the Penns decided to settle the argument by one stroke of autocracy—they extinguished "all Indian titles to Pennsylvania."[2] This aroused indignation and resentment in the Indians, who "said they were cheated . . . they felt excused from fulfilling the obligations they had assumed to William Penn and the Quakers," and so "joined heartily with the French in their hostilities."[3]

By the year 1745 the Six Nations were being pressed by all the colonies to make war on the French. The Quaker tradition expressed still in the Pennsylvanian Assembly (by a majority in it) had counteracted any military schemes so far, and the Iroquois had supported this policy.

But the Delawares grew unsettled, unrest was evident in many directions; they were suppressed by the Six Nations; they had lost confidence in the English;

[1] See Appendix IV.   [2] Sharpless. Op. cit., p. 176.
[3] Ib., pp. 176-7.

rumours were wild and rife that armies were surrounding them; there was no hope of redress from the Council or Assembly. The Supply Bill was another source of grievance, as the Penns were excusing themselves from paying their share of this tax on the proprietary lands. The Assembly and Council grew alienated, and in an endeavour to mediate between them a commission was appointed to administrate public monies. The Assembly had grown doubtful of the integrity and wisdom of the Council (as instanced in their dealing with the proprietaries) and had consequently decided to supply arms secretly to the colonists on the border. War was being waged, unofficially, in these areas, much scalping and pillaging being indulged in, resulting in whole districts being laid waste. The next step was to erect a complete chain of forts along the frontier from Easton to Maryland. The Council followed up this act of defence by an act of aggression—war was declared against the Delaware Indians (April 1756) and as a necessary corollary to such a procedure, the scalping bounty offered one hundred and thirty Spanish dollars for every male Indian scalp over twelve years of age and fifty dollars for every female. A strong Quaker element in the Council, led by James Logan, powerfully and persuasively opposed such measures, as being abhorrent to them, but without success. However, "the plan of defense by a line of forts; the expenditure of over £50,000; the arming of over one thousand men; the bounty on Indian scalps; all these things were of no avail in protecting the frontier. The stealthy savage in the dead hours of the night, or at high noon, fell upon the inhabitants in the least suspected quarter. Pennsylvania was saturated in blood.

Whole settlements were destroyed. Fire and plunder, death and murder flourished in the teeth of all opposition. For over seventy-five years Pennsylvania had lived in peace with the Indians. Now, when war rages along her border, it was not so much her defenses as her peace negotiations which won protection for her people. . . . The greatest victories which Pennsylvania ever won in this French and Indian war were victories of peace."[1]

The Friends continued to work untiringly in the cause of peace. They offered the Council to act as mediators and pressed for forgiveness of all past offences with the return of prisoners. They volunteered large sums of money for use by the Governor in lieu of the war-tax demanded, and through the Friendly Association expended about 25,000 dollars in measures for their ideal; they assisted the Indians very materially in their distress, and took care to be present at all times when treaties were being considered, in order to ensure the rightful treatment of the Indians. They secured a Peace Pact for them in 1757, mainly achieved by the efforts of Christian Frederic Post, a Moravian missionary, working for their Association. Encouraged by confidence in the Quaker principles, Teedyuscung, 'King of the Delawares,' went up and down among his people as far as the Wyoming territory, persuading them to bury the hatchet and accept the offer of conference with the Six Nations, preliminary to establishing a general peace. Such was his success that the tribes met at Easton, where all past grievances were exposed. After much argument and many difficult

[1] Joseph S. Walton. *Conrad Weiser and the Indian Policy of Colonial Pennsylvania.* Philadelphia, 1900 (pp. 325-326).

proposals a settlement was agreed upon in 1758. Prisoners were returned and all decided to make every effort to maintain a state of amity and concord (1758). Ten years later the territories of Red Man and White Man were geographically divided. In 1776 Pennsylvania became a commonwealth, whereby the Quakers were deprived of any share in governmental authority. The year 1784 witnessed the purchase of all the remaining north-western region by the State. "With the birth of the Federal Government"[1] (1787) of which Philadelphia was the capital, Pennsylvania widened her borders and separated herself entirely from the Indians and their affairs.

[1] Ib., p. 390.

Chapter VI

ACTUAL GOVERNMENT

"Whose Children are they who break the Peace of Nations, Communities and Families?"—THOMAS CHALKLEY.

WILLIAM PENN's ideals when colonising Pennsylvania were "the best and most exalted that could occupy the human mind, namely, to render men as free and as happy as the nature of their existence could possibly bear in their capacity."[1] With what success subsequent history shows; his name is held in love and honour, as one who achieved for his people "one of the happiest places that have ever existed as the home of man on the restless planet,"[2] with "a sense of security . . . taxes . . . comparatively nothing . . . no internal broils, . . . no persecution for religion, . . . a land . . . of plenty, flowing, as it were, with milk and honey."[3] "Being divinely qualified, he was a very able and excellent instrument in the hand of Providence in removing much of that superstitious bigotry and ignorance, which for ages had overspread . . . the minds of all ranks of people. . . . If the fable of the golden age was ever verified or a paradoxical State introduced on earth . . . they must have borne the nearest resemblance to that of Pennsylvania."[4]

The granting of the territory by Charles II, the

[1] Proud. (Quoted by Clarkson, p. 97.)
[2] John W. Graham. Op. cit., p. 284.   [3] Clarkson. Op. cit., p. 367.
[4] Proud. Op. cit., vol. ii, p. 106-7.

signing of the Charter for its Government, Penn's journey to the New World, the establishment there of a Council and Assembly, with himself as Proprietary, in accordance with his aspirations for a truly democratic State, were but initial steps towards the great Ideal. The project, however, could not be fulfilled apart from its association with the Home Country. English authority was paramount, and the affairs of Friends in his own land called Penn away from the young colony as soon as ever he could possibly be spared. It was very early days for inexperienced 'children' in the art of the new statecraft to be left dependent upon their own judgment and discretion. At times they paid dearly for their learning, but their response to liberty, and their freedom from suppressions or wars made them a very happy, prosperous community. So Penn confidently gave them the reins of government, and in August 1684, came back to the trouble and persecution in England. Rumours regarding his own integrity whilst abroad were silenced by a dignified refutation of them; the question of boundaries, still rankling between himself and Lord Baltimore, was dealt with by the Committee of Trade and Plantations; Penn's claim was granted and his opponent pacified. The next problem, to which he could now wholeheartedly devote himself, was that of the ill-treated and imprisoned Friends. As many as 1,400 people are said to have been in gaol at the time of the accession of James II. The gentle Quaker politician, courtly, yet humble; wise, yet with a simple faith; gracious, though strong to oppose tyranny, and ever eager that humanity should progress along the way of uplift and freedom, won the confidence and friendship of the new sovereign.

His popularity aided his purpose considerably: people
in need flocked to him with their grievances, and in
just over a year he succeeded in obtaining from the
King "a general pardon to all who were in prison on
account of conscientious dissent . . . among them
upwards of thirteen hundred Friends."[1]   When lives
were lost in the Monmouth rebellion and Judge
Jefferies added to the number by convicting political
insurgents, who were to be hanged or transported,
William Penn protested vigorously against such
atrocities.   He "begged twenty"[2] from James of the
thousand men to be exiled and shipped them to the
pleasant land of Pennsylvania.[3]

Activities of a similar nature occupied his attention
for the next few years, not only in England but abroad,
where he went to fulfil a great desire to re-visit his
friends to whom he had fled in his youth.   Whilst in
Holland he also had audience of Prince William of
Orange, pleading his cause with him; thence proceeding
to Germany, "refreshing the spirits"[4] of his Quaker
brethren.   His return was to a much perturbed and
disquieted England.   James II was weak and was
constantly attempting measures which destroyed confidence in him.   As his intimate counsellor and adviser,
Penn urged the king to grant religious freedom to *all*
his people, including Roman Catholics.   Instead of
acceding to this request, in a constitutional act, James
autocratically granted toleration through his royal

---

[1] Janney. Op. cit., p. 281.   [2] Ib., p. 268.
[3] This insurrection, with the Quaker reaction to all it involved, led
to misleading accusations and false charges—the most serious being
those of Thomas B. Macaulay.   The reader is asked to examine these
separately, as they are entirely beyond the scope of the present work.
[4] Stoughton. Op. cit., p. 232.

prerogative, and issued the *Declaration of Indulgence*. This annoyed almost every religious sect and every political faction: it led to the trial and imprisonment of the Seven Bishops, who considered it a step towards papistry. Penn, who really pleaded for the release of the prelates, and objected to James' methods, yet became 'suspect' amongst all classes in England as a Jesuit and false prophet. His position was not enviable; he yearned for Pennsylvania, where the young State needed him sadly "to compose their bickerings and suppress their factions by his commanding prestige and tactful will";[1] yet how leave England! Rumours and imputations against him had made him highly unpopular; the things he so much wanted for his people had a tremendous price in the opposition of an orthodox nation; the Quakers themselves pressed for his presence here. Furthermore, he had a great persuasion towards getting complete religious liberty established in England; then all must surely be well with Pennsylvania! Meanwhile, ecclesiasts and politicians were so exasperated by James II, that they opened negotiations with William of Orange, and in 1688 the Whig Party sent an invitation to him to come and be king. He came, "not as a conqueror" of the land, but "as a protector of the Protestant religion, and in order to secure the liberty of the subject."[2] James fled; William and Mary reigned in his stead.

William was "a soldier and a fighter first, statesman and diplomatist afterwards, . . . subtle, adroit and

---

[1] Augustus C. Buell. *William Penn as the Founder of Two Commonwealths.* By permission of D. Appleton-Century Company, Inc., owners of the copyright.
[2] Janney. Op. cit., p. 347.

far-seeing."[1] Even as Prince of Orange he had voiced
his contempt for the "so-called scruple of the Quakers
against force of arms. He said it was a doctrine without
sanction of any law in statute or in morals, human or
divine. . . .   This was a doctrine he would never
defend; those who pretended to believe it placed themselves without the pale of protection by laws which
they refused to enforce." As King of England he made
it quite clear that as far as he was concerned, the only
accredited form of rule was that wherein the Government had complete control, including the regularising
of religious practices: he believed "that in religion, as
in all other human concerns, there was need of law,
order and dispensation, . . . or mankind must become
a mob and society a rabble."[2]

The *Toleration Act* of 1689 met the demands of King
and people in granting freedom of worship and opinions
to individuals, whilst retaining for the partisans of the
Crown all constitutional offices. An appeal for the
abolition of the tests was treated by compromise;
Roman Catholics were excluded from Parliament, but
granted liberty of worship, and members of the Society
of Friends were permitted to give a promise of loyalty
to the sovereign instead of the oath—which was impossible for them. To Penn this Bill brought the reward
for twenty years of patient endeavour and earnest
striving—the first great step towards perfect liberty of
conscience. His own tribulations were by no means
ended yet; accusations with intent to convict and
imprison him seemed to beset his path. He was brought
to trial for treasonable correspondence with James; he

[1] Buell. Op. cit., p. 201.
[2] Ib. Op. cit., pp. 187-8.

was included in Queen Mary's list of eighteen who were "disaffected to the government" [1] during William's absence in Ireland; an impostor "had under oath accused him to the government." [2] None of these charges was proved against him, but they were burdensome and troublesome to him. The predominant wish in Penn's heart at this time was to get back to Pennsylvania, whence reports came continually of problems needing to be solved, of difficulties in administrative technique, and a tendency to general demoralisation for want of its chief. "There is nothing that my soul breathes more for in this world . . . than that I may see poor Pennsylvania again . . . but I cannot force my way hence," [3] he wrote to his steward. So strong was the urge within him that he had agreed to accept a convoy provided and pressed upon him by the State for his safe crossing, but this project had to be abandoned. There was no other course open to him than to retire from public life into a secluded residence, in London, concealed from opponents and friends alike. In this quiet estate he wrote an *Epistle General to the People of God, called Quakers* (really a vindication of his own conduct); and a letter to Thomas Lloyd, President of the Council in Pennsylvania, explaining his absence. It was a great testing of his faith, but he humbly submitted to the will of God, whereby he might be better fitted for His work, growing greater in wisdom and stronger in fervour to be the instrument of the Lord.

The colony of Pennsylvania had been left to its own

---

[1] Janney. Op. cit., p. 361.

[2] Ib. Op. cit., p. 361.

[3] Ib. Op. cit., p. 285 (Letter to J. Harrison).

devices, under a Deputy-Governor, in its very young days. Only urgent necessity kept Penn away: he knew of the many bickerings and difficulties among the rulers, over matters both petty and important, and the inefficiency of a company of tyros, without the guiding hand which might have steered them amicably through the troubled waters.

One of the chief occasions of unrest in the early years of the experiment was what is known as the Keithian controversy, which seriously divided and disturbed the Pennsylvania Friends. George Keith, a Scotsman, had been appointed headmaster of the first public school established in the city of Philadelphia "for the training and instruction of children of both sexes in the useful arts and sciences." He was much respected, and had accompanied Penn on his travels in Germany. But he appears to have been quick-tempered, over-bearing, and fond of disputations, and one of his contentions was that the use of force in support of supposed justice was unjustifiable. Another of his arguments which rendered him unpopular among his Quaker brethren was that the Inward Light was not necessary for salvation. He was arraigned before their Monthly Meeting, which only served to exasperate him further and drew from him bitter and disrespectful language. The Yearly Meeting of 1692 disowned him, and a declaration, or testimony of denial, was drawn up and signed by twenty-eight of the most important members and confirmed by 214 more.

This religious schism became later a matter of civil concern. When a small sloop had been stolen from the wharf at Philadelphia by a pirate who was apprehended and brought to trial, Keith declared himself against such an act of magistracy as contrary to the principles of the Quakers with regard to the use of force. He is said to have made use of "insulting and threatening language against the Governor." Keith and one of his friends then published a defence under the title of *Plea of the Innocent*, in which they personally abused Samuel Jennings, one of the judges. They were brought before the Court and adjudged to pay each a fine of five pounds, but the fines were never exacted. Keith and his adherents complained of religious persecution, but he remained two years longer in the country with his separate congregation and afterwards went to England, where he obtained a curacy in the Church. Subsequently he returned with the alleged object of making proselytes to the High Church from among the colonists.[1]

Notwithstanding these dissensions and some confusion in the government, the population of the State was contented and satisfied, enjoying liberty and prospering in a productive land under quite happy circumstances.[2] But a new authority arose in England; French aggression grew imminent; the danger of the colony of Peace being made a bone of contention between France and England loomed as a possibility in the near future; schism in the country itself, both political and religious, sprang into being, and the fate

[1] See Ebeling in Hazard's *Register*, I, p. 371.
[2] The impressions of at least one contemporary colonist have been preserved. Gabriel Thomas wrote in 1698 *An Account of Pennsylvania and West New Jersey*, and dedicated it to "William Penn Most Noble and Excellent Governor." It is signed "Thy hearty Well-wisher ever ready to serve thee on all occasions in the way of truth." He declared that "I must needs say, even the present Encouragements are very great and inviting, for poor People (both men and women) of all kinds, can get here three times the wages for their labour than in England or Wales" (p. 40).

E—P

of Pennsylvania hung in the balance. Confidence in
the non-resistance policy which was the principle of its
foundation was being shaken by rumours of probable
invasions, of pressure being brought to bear upon it
which could not be withstood, and fear began to creep
into the hearts of the colonists that they might be
overwhelmed and destroyed. By 1692, 4,000 out of
12,000 were prepared to join the militia in preference
to paying the poll-tax. A state of war between the
home-land and France had been a menace since 1689,
when all territories in America had been warned "to
take prompt and efficient measures"[1] against invasion.
Captain John Blackwell was at the head of affairs,
having been chosen, perhaps unwisely, as a governor
who did not belong to the Society of Friends. His
conduct, therefore, in the matter of defence was not
as scrupulously non-militant as that of a Quaker.
Accordingly he "recommended the enrolment of a
provincial militia for defense, as was done in all other
colonies."[2] This proposal was "received with derision"
by the Assembly and "treated with contempt."[3]

Efforts to persuade these people to take action against
anyone, for any reason, even in self-defence, signally
failed. When William III had sent two Dutch officials
to report to him on Pennsylvania, they had brought
back word "first, that the colonists were not prepared
for any kind of attack; second, that they could not be
induced to prepare; and, third, that if attacked they
would have to be defended either by royal forces from
England or by the militia of New York and Maryland."[4]
To show his impatience with this attitude, the King

---

[1] Buell. Op. cit., p. 227.　　[2] Ib. Op. cit., p. 227.
[3] Ib. Op. cit., p. 227.　　[4] Ib. Op. cit., p. 211.

suspended their Executive Council and placed the
State under the command of Colonel Benjamin Fletcher,
Governor of New York, with full power to take whatever steps he decided to be necessary to ensure adequate
defence for the colony and her boundaries. New York
itself had quite recently been a victim of the war-
mongering which was part of French policy; continual
efforts were made to ally the Indians with themselves,
and, with the moral support of the home countries'
state of war, to encroach upon English lands to their
ultimate absorption. Colonel Fletcher was, to some
extent, therefore, justified in his fear for Pennsylvania.
With almost unrestricted power (even to the proposal
from William of placing the colony under martial law
if it opposed him) Fletcher immediately proceeded to
Philadelphia, ousted the Council and convened the
Assembly, to whom he expounded his scheme. Money
must be raised for purposes of defence. Rather than
that they be dispersed the members of the Assembly
gave in. One form of levy—that of the poll-tax—could
be evaded by joining the militia. Strange as it may
seem, even the 'soldier-William', who had little or no
sympathy with religion, and certainly none with those
who preferred peace to any form of war, made no
attempt to press the Quakers into military action—the
'Inward Light' of these disciples of George Fox was
respected. Such men did not share the Colonel's
apprehensions "that the Province was in danger of
being lost to the Crown, although the government was
in the hands of some whose principles were not for
war."[1] William's intent to provoke the colonists into
some show of antagonism or desire for their own

[1] Clarkson. Op. cit., p. 235.

protection, was frustrated by the stolid refusal of the Friends to acquiesce in any attempt at warlike measures: they stipulated that monies paid by them to government were for purposes of administration and not to be 'dipped in blood.' Neither would they be hoodwinked into paying taxes—ostensibly to supply the Indians with necessities in order to guarantee their friendship—but actually for the army, as they realised when a second demand was made in 1694 by Fletcher, whose coercive attitude proved utterly futile. In August of that year William, grasping the significance of the situation, restored Penn to the Proprietorship.[1] Letters patent were granted and an instrument was drafted, whereby Penn had his beloved colony again put into his possession, with an admission from the King concerning the 'grave miscarriages' there "*that the disorder and confusion* into which the Province and territories had fallen, *had been occasioned entirely by his absence from them.*"[2] The death of his wife upset his plans for an immediate journey to Pennsylvania. Markham was appointed Lieutenant-Governor instead. He pursued the policy of Fletcher and convened the Assembly only. Without its consent he dissolved both Council and Assembly. A great remonstrance was made against such an arbitrary proceeding, which resulted in Markham granting special privileges of a conciliatory nature to the Assembly, one of which was "being authorised to

[1] This had been taken from him by Mary during William's absence in Ireland. Hazard's *Register* of August 16th, 1828 (vol. ii, p. 71) contains a copy of Queen Mary's Letter to William Penn, restoring his authority. In this she writes of Penn's "good assurance" that he would "take care of the government . . . and provide for the safety and security thereof all that in you lies" and goes on to revoke the appointment of Fletcher.
[2] Clarkson Op. Cit., p. 240.

originate bills"—in entire opposition to the constitutional principles of its founder, and never formally sanctioned by him. (The Assembly used it, however, until 1700). To show its appreciation of its improved status, a bill was introduced undertaking to raise £300 for the relief of distressed Indians.

The management of this experimental domain was not a simple affair. Penn himself had to be in England and rule his colony through deputies, who were not always in agreement with his views; nor did they always use his methods. Pennsylvania was intended to be a free democracy, whereas it was actually a feudal holding. The English Crown was always the supreme authority: the very title of Proprietary could be vested in some one else whenever an English sovereign chose. William had, already, once appointed one of his own partisans as Governor, Colonel Fletcher, who demanded "a quota of 80 men, with their officers, or the expense of maintaining such a body . . . to be available from Pennsylvania for the use of New York. Fletcher applied for the 80 men in April 1695. They were to be at Albany as soon as possible after 21st May."[1] *But they were not there!* The grant of money by the Assembly under Markham seems a compromise, but things had to be worked in this way. Penn realised that unless he were prepared to lose his treasured colony altogether and with it his cherished ideal, he must come to some sort of terms and understanding with the British Government: recognise Pennsylvania as part of its Empire and get for her the best conditions possible against the odds of a warlike nation.

The benefits accruing from the staunch adherence to

[1] J. W. Graham Op. Cit., p. 224.

the principles of peace in this young, isolated territory are shown clearly in the words of Colonel Fletcher himself, in spite of his former fears concerning her welfare and safety from invasion. Of the capital of this defenceless country he wrote in 1696, "Philadelphia in fourteen years time is become equal to the city of New York in trade and riches, so that many people have gone to Philadelphia to enjoy their ease and avoid the hardship of defending New York, and there being free trade in Philadelphia business had gone there."[1] For five years after the re-instatement of Penn with his policy of religious freedom and fearless refusal of war "the colonists of Pennsylvania enjoyed a degree of prosperity and happiness that seldom falls to the lot of humanity."[2] The excellence of the constitution made Pennsylvania "the most consistently free colony in the country, the most consistently prosperous . . . and so nearly had the inhabitants everything they could desire that they hesitated to take up the revolutionary cause in 1775."[3]

Throughout his career, almost from his boyhood, Penn had been called to make great decisions. In Ireland, as early as 1665, he was offered a commission in the army, which he refused in order to preach the gospel. Two years later he had to leave either his 'persuasion in the Quaker doctrine' or his father's home. He left his home. In England he might have settled down to a life of luxury as a wealthy country gentleman or a statesman with social prestige, but he preferred to work in Pennsylvania, 'sent thither by the Lord.' In William's accession to the English throne there was

---

[1] Quoted by J. W. Graham. Op. cit., p. 225.
[2] Janney. Op. 397.   [3] Sharpless. Op. cit., p. 55.

a grave menace to the land of his dreams. This king intended to bring it under normal jurisdiction. It actually belonged to him, and Penn must choose "between the legitimate demands of the government and the legitimate principles of the Quaker Colony."[1] It could only be done by compromise, and he made the sacrifice in order to preserve intact the constitution of his precious province. 'The great call' impelled him in each case to choose the path of self-denial and high endeavour—to fulfil the law of God in a work of love for humanity, serving it and saving it, to the utmost of his capacity. With each decision there seemed to come a special adversity: the death of his father, wife, and son weighing him with sorrow, added to his tribulation. Long confinements were imposed upon him, when, cut off from intercourse with people he communed with his God, and wrote his messages for the guidance of those whose interests he ever had at heart. His *Fruits of Solitude* was a compendium of the wisdom gained by years of experience in the service of the children of this world, and *An Essay towards the Present and Future Peace of Europe* set forth "the desirableness of peace and the truest means of it: to wit, justice, and not war."[2] A great blessing was vouchsafed to him in Hannah Callowhill, his second wife (married 1696) a veritable tower of strength, beloved by all whom she met and with a reasonable amount of wealth to assist him in his return to Pennsylvania.

While Markham was struggling vainly to "govern the ungovernable"[3] people in Pennsylvania, who refused to make a reasonable opposition (in the way of

---

[1] J. W. Graham. Op. cit., p. 222. [2] Janney. Op. cit., p. 384.
[3] Buell. Op. cit., p. 241.

armed force) to piracy, smuggling and threats of invasion, Penn, in England, occupied himself with various problems which were presented by the system of Quakerism in an unsympathetic world; visiting and comforting the afflicted, interviewing influential authorities, addressing meetings, and writing religious pamphlets. But a growing resentment against the form of rule in the New World territory was causing a sense of insecurity concerning it. William felt that something must be done about it and Colonel Quarry,[1] his representative in the province, was using all his powers to make the Quaker experiment a failure. By the autumn of 1699 William appears to have been only too ready and willing to send Penn out again to "put his house in order"[2] there. This he undertook to do. He was greeted with enthusiasm and a feeling of great relief. Markham welcomed his coming "as a prisoner in a dungeon might hail the tidings of release";[3] the inhabitants rejoiced as children who desired the paternal presence of their benevolent, reliable, illustrious founder. Confidence was re-established as they saw Penn and his family alight from the ship *Canterbury* to come to stay amongst them. Yet the wise ruler knew that these men must learn to rely upon their own judgment, make their own decisions, and administer their own democracy. He convened the Assembly to place before them two bills—one to suppress piracy,[4] the other to prevent

[1] Quarry's charges and Penn's reply are reprinted from the *Memoirs* of the Historical Society of Pennsylvania in Hazard's *Register*, vol. viii, p. 218.   [2] Buell.   [3] Ib.

[4] A letter from William Blathwayt to Abraham Hill, written from Diexen, August 21st, 1699, alleged that "grievous complaints had been made against Pennsilvania in respect of the pirates," and it is suggested that the authorities might not be wholly free from guilt in regard to the continuance of a practice which was greatly to the disadvantage of

illicit trade, that is, smuggling. Both were made constitutional Acts as Penn was "very zealous and willing to do all things to promote the King's interests" [1] and to keep his province a law-abiding, moral, and efficient State. "Abuses were checked with a strong hand; . . . acquiescence in evil when the means were at hand to strike it down morally never was a part of their (the Quakers') principles or practice." [2]

The Governor at this time resided at Pennsbury where, with Hannah, his wife, he kept "open house and dispensed a stately hospitality to all comers, rich or poor, high or low, white or red alike." [3] A new Council and Assembly were elected and they met in April 1700 to discuss the possibility of a new Charter. Penn in his opening address invited them "to read the charter and frame of government, to keep what is good, in either, to lay aside what is inconvenient and burdensome, and to add to both what may best suit the common good." [4] No agreement could be reached as to the terms of a new charter and dissatisfaction

the province and its inhabitants. The writer of the letter asks the question, "Will not every governor be willing enough to be turned out when he has made his fortune by these pirates?" In a letter to Colonel Nicolson, the Governor of Maryland, Penn expressed his abhorrence of such methods as that of "conniving at forbidden Trade, or the abuse of the Crown in a lawful one." And he adds that "if any are faulty in my propriety, as I am innocent so I am sure I would not endure but punish it to extremity, if among them." Of the pirates themselves two most notorious ones were Captain Kidd, and an individual who appears to have been well known to the people of Philadelphia, and to have been called Captain Teach or, more popularly, Blackbeard. According to J. F. Watson he was in reality a native of Bristol, named Drummond, "a half-crazed man in high excitements by his losses and imprisonments from the French." (*Annals of Philadelphia*, vol. ii, p. 221.)

[1] Stoughton. Op. cit., p. 299.
[2] Sharpless. Op. cit., p. 463.
[3] Buell. Op. cit., p. 247.
[4] Janney. Op. cit., p. 246.

with the old one was most evident, so Penn decided
the matter by putting before them, for their acceptance,
the letters patent of William (1699). Very soon,
however, he had again to call them together to consider
a demand from the Home Government for £350 to
build forts along the frontier of New York. After four
days of "unpleasant parley" over this embarrassing
situation, the Assembly wrote down their decision to do
what the King required of them *as far as their religious
scruples would permit*. One fervent old Quaker, Claypole,
stated, "rather than vote a farthing for the wicked uses
of war" he "would see the province ravaged by French
pirates from the ocean or massacred by French Indians
from Canada. It would only be persecution for righteousness' sake, and Friends knew how to suffer that."[1]
Penn accepted this attitude, but within a fortnight
another assembly had to be convened: things were
happening in England which necessitated Penn's immediate presence there—a Bill had been introduced in
the House of Lords by Lord Ranelagh to revoke his
charter and incorporate Pennsylvania as a representative Crown Colony. Before leaving the country he
desired to establish a government to carry on his work.
This he arranged by the use of letters patent according
to his proclamation the previous spring (1701). A
Council of State was appointed with a Governor and
eight officials to act in his absence and the Assembly
was privileged, among other concessions, to the power
of originating bills. This new charter was in "every
part thereof approved, agreed to and thankfully
received."[2] Almost immediately he set sail for England,

[1] Buell. Op. cit., p. 252.
[2] *Colonial Records*. Quoted by Janney. Op. cit., p. 451.

where he expected to settle the dispute concerning his property in person and quickly. But Hannah found it wise to accompany him, and once in the home-land circumstances contrived to make their return impossible. Two influential lords (Romney and Rochester) were personal friends of Penn and brought about the withdrawal of Lord Ranelagh's bill. In about two months' time a similar bill was introduced in Parliament, promoted secretly by the King. While under discussion, a fatal accident to William removed the initiator of the scheme to abolish proprietary government and make uniform the direct authority of the English Crown; so the matter lapsed. The attitude of Queen Anne, daughter of James II, was one of complete sympathy with the Society of Friends, personal intimacy with Penn, and ready acquiescence in the method of government in Pennsylvania. She acceded to the throne at a period when war was being waged between England and France. Marlborough, her adviser, was a militant statesman, who believed in armed forces for colonies as well as countries and their control by the British Sovereign. Penn had installed Andrew Hamilton as Governor with James Logan as his own personal representative in the American State: Marlborough did not approve but was over ruled by Anne. In 1703 Hamilton died, and the question of a new successor was long debated. With great reluctance and without admitting the true state of affairs to his colonists, Penn agreed to the appointment of John Evans by the Crown. He was accepted and recommended to Logan as "a young man . . . sober and sensible . . . discreet and advisable . . . by the best of our friends."[1] His

[1] Janney. Op. cit., p. 474.

simple faith in human beings misled Penn, often with disastrous results.[1] Evans was an officer of militia, full of enthusiasm, but with little balanced judgment, eager to show how well he could equip the Province and make strong her self-defence. He issued a proclamation as his very first act of presumed authority, calling on all citizens to form a militia. The 'overseers of the press' (Quakers) refused to print it. He had it printed at his own expense. There were 26,000 white people in Pennsylvania, about 9,000 of them in Philadelphia. For some years past a considerable influx of emigrants from various countries in Europe had tended to swell the numbers of non-Quakers in the colony: they were Swiss, German, Huguenot and Scottish-Irish,[2] so that Evans found a land with many ready to join him in forming an army. The non-militant element had only a small majority in Philadelphia (5,000 to 4,000) and a similar proportion in the province. The Delaware territory provided the greater part of the ten companies who responded to his appeal. Enraged at the scantiness

[1] But Penn had written in a letter to Friends in Pennsylvania dated 24th of 9th month, 1694: "We must creep where we cannot go, and it is necessary for us in the things of this world to be wise as to be innocent."

[2] In his book called *The Struggle in America between England and France*, 1697-1763 Justin Winsor says: "Along the Pennsylvanian border, the Scotch Irish were receiving new currents of their valiant blood. This North Irish people had been paid for their devotion to the Protestant succession in England by so much persecution for their conformity that they had sought relief by coming to the American colonies in large numbers. . . . In 1724-5 three thousand of them are said to have landed in Philadelphia. It was computed that in the single year 1729 five thousand of them entered Pennsylvania. This great influx put the Quaker element in a decided minority, but it was many years later before the Society of Friends ceased to have a predominant power in the political machinery of the province. Already James Logan, representing the Conservative Quakers, was looking to Parliament for relief from what seemed an impending inundation of this hardy stock" (p. 166).

of the forces he had collected, Evans dissolved the Assembly and issued writs for a new election. At their meeting the Quakers still refused to specify that any money voted by them should be used for the equipment of an army. They granted part to the Governor for purposes of organisation and part to the Queen. All his arguments and threats of the Crown's resorting to measures such as had been enforced under Fletcher, were of no avail. He still made a big effort to carry out his scheme: he completed the fort at New Castle and armed his six hundred militia-men. He was convinced of the necessity to show the Pennsylvanians the danger they were placing themselves in by remaining defence-less against the privateers and pirates who infested the American coast and were causing great poverty to the Province by their depredations. He quoted to them the case of De Castries, an enterprising young French officer, who, in April 1706, commanded a squadron of four fast-sailing frigates, fitted out and sent to cruise off Long Island. This warlike sailor decided to scare the people of the coastal regions. There were not many British ships in evidence in these waters; two small corvettes were guarding the Delaware capes. These De Castries chased up the bay, almost to New Castle. He "landed at Lewes for wood, water and fresh provisions, *but did not molest the inhabitants* except to take away some of their livestock."[1] Real apprehension lest he should take advantage of the unprotected Delaware estuary to venture to attack Philadelphia, prompted Evans to test the non-militant population he was trying to govern.

A favourable opportunity presented itself in the

[1] Buell. Op. cit., p. 271. Italics mine.

gathering together of the people for a fair. Evans wrote a letter purporting to be from the Governor of Maryland, whose signature he forged, addressed to himself at New Castle. Instructions were given for any letter arriving there to be delivered to him in Philadelphia immediately. Messengers obeyed this order and duly presented the missive. With dramatic effect Evans called a council to hear it, and decided to proclaim the news to the whole population. To add weight to this scare of an invasion the Sheriff of New Castle had been ordered to raise an alarm. The letter announced the near approach of the French squadron into the Delaware. The recent landing at Lewes was exaggerated into a tale of burning the town and ravaging the whole settlement. As a brand to the fire he was lighting the Governor mounted his horse and rode excitedly through the town, brandishing his sword and calling all men to arms—ready for the foe who *might* arrive at Society Hill! There "nearly seven hundred able-bodied men assembled . . . with any sort of weapons they could find and demanded to be led against the invaders."[1] Four only of these were Quakers, who were later ostracised by the Society. No other Friend attempted to bear arms. They fled to the woods with their wives and children, but, "not a Friend of any note but behaved as becomes our profession."[2] The whole proceeding was discovered by James Logan to be a false alarm, a preconcerted attempt to drive the Quakers from their principles: such a shallow artifice to trick them and force them into a compromising position, roused widespread indignation against Evans, and availed him nothing.

[1] Buell. Op. cit., p. 273.   [2] Ib., p. 274.

Further unscrupulous conduct was exhibited in his restriction of the freedom of the waters of the Delaware. The Charter stipulated the unmolested passage of all ships; but Evans placed a commander in charge of his newly-armed fort at New Castle, to hail all ships, and to exact from the inward-bound a tax of 'half a pound of powder for every ton weight.' This unjust imposition caused much resentment amongst traders, and three Friends decided to ignore the signal whereby they should report. Richard Hill and two companions just steered past, with no more hurt than a shot in one sail. French, the commandant of the fort, pursued in an armed boat; he was inveigled on board the recalcitrant sloop; conveyed to Salem and brought before the vice-admiral of the Delaware. He severely reprimanded French, then dismissed him, at the same time sending an expression of disapprobation of his whole scheme to Governor Evans. This act of Richard Hill broke down completely the whole system of false impositions, and re-established navigation in the estate granted by the Charter.

During the early years of Evans' rule the Assembly had gone on its peaceful way, busily attending to the administration of the country which enjoyed a period of harmony and contented prosperity. As many as fifty bills were brought in and passed during one single session. The trouble began when Evans succeeded in stirring up warfare. The bitter opposition he aroused resulted in appeal after appeal from the colonists to Penn, to recall him. As this was outside his jurisdiction (a fact not realised in Pennsylvania), he had to look on, powerless to help his people out of the miserable state of turmoil and poverty that the coercive governor had brought about. One point at least was clear to him and consoled his conscience—it was quite evident that his ideal policy of peace for the province was the right and only way to secure happiness and well-being.

In 1709 Colonel Charles Gookin was appointed to succeed Governor Evans. He exerted his influence towards the return of tranquillity and progress. But the Home Government did not leave him long undisturbed. Frequent demands were made of the Assembly for money. First they were asked to pay taxes for armies of defence, then in 1709 to pay their quota towards a project of the Queen's, to fit out an expedition for the retaking of Newfoundland, and for the conquest of Canada. Gookin assured them that this time it was no false alarm, and pressed them to comply. The Quaker element overruled him, and refused to raise money to hire men to fight or kill one another; but they would make a present to the Queen of £500. In 1711 another demand of the same nature, another attempt of Gookin to persuade them to accede, resulted in the same reply being made by the Assembly: they would not raise money for purposes of killing one another. Gookin argued that the Queen "did not hire men to kill one another but to destroy her enemies."[1] One of the Assembly was thereby provoked to remark that "the Assembly understood English."[2] They presented the Queen with £2,000, as "a testimony of their loyalty and in gratitude for her many favours." The poverty which had been experienced by the Colony, as the direct outcome of William's wars, had left Penn almost destitute in England, and as he had

[1] Sharpless. Op. cit., p. 201.
[2] Ib. Op. cit., do.

very little business ability, his affairs and estates were
placed under the management of Philip Ford—a
Quaker and lawyer whom Penn trusted implicitly, but
who proved himself utterly unworthy, a presumptuous
man and a cheat. He went so far as to proclaim Penn
to be indebted to him for £10,500. The matter was
kept quiet during his life-time by calling the sum a
mortgage on the Pennsylvanian territory. At Ford's
death the widow and son openly declared Penn bank-
rupt, and got him imprisoned for debt whence he was
incapable of procuring his liberty for nine months.
Friends then paid enough to satisfy the Fords, who
were claiming the colony as their possession. For
some time Penn had been endeavouring to raise money
on his Charter grant, but he would not sell to the
Government except on his own terms. He refused to
run any risks of jeopardising the hard-won religious
liberty of Quakers in Pennsylvania; he insisted on
provisions ensuring freedom for all immigrants, which
had been his purpose in founding the State. Miserable,
poor, in prison, and an ailing man, he yet fought in
his righteous cause with the old fervour of the zealous
Friend. His release enabled him to press his suit further
—but in the midst of negotiations with Queen Anne
he was stricken with paralysis, so that nothing more
could be done. Hence his proprietary rights and his
estates in America remained to him and his widow
Hannah and their descendents until the year of
Revolution, 1776, when their interests were vested in
the Commonwealth.

The sickness which attacked Penn in Fleet prison
left him a disabled man in the political and commercial
world. Gradually he grew weaker and more retiring,

till finally he settled to a few years of well-earned peace, enjoying the fruits of the renewed prosperity of Pennsylvania, in his quiet country home at Ruscombe, where his brilliant but chequered career was laid aside (1718). Hannah travelled on through the "woods and wildernesses of this world,"[1] without her guide for several years.

William Penn was "a man of great abilities, of an excellent sweetness of disposition . . . full of the qualification of true discipleship, even love without dissimulation . . . so ready to forgive enemies that the ungrateful were not excepted . . . learned, good and great . . . weighty and serious . . . of an extraordinary greatness of mind, yet void of the stain of ambition . . . a man, a scholar, a friend, a minister surpassing in superlative endowments, whose memorial will be valued by the wise and blessed with the just."[2]

[1] Stoughton. Op. cit., p. 358.
[2] Ib., pp. 356-7. A tribute of Reading Friends at their monthly meeting.

Chapter VII

THE END OF THE HOLY EXPERIMENT

"The non-violent resister returns good for evil, not because he is a weakling, but because he believes that the unity of mankind is the most important thing in the world and that such action is the most efficient means of maintaining what he believes in" namely "spiritual equality, . . . that all men have the dignity of sons of God."

"It is said that non-violent resistance is a surrender of the right of self-defence. Not so. It changes radically the method of defence and perhaps somewhat enlarges the conception of the self, but the defence is still there, active, alert and effective."—RICHARD B. GREGG. *The Power of Non-violence.*[1]

"Men must be holy or they cannot be happy, . . . they should be few in words, peaceable in life, suffer wrongs, love enemies, deny themselves . . . worship God . . . and bring forth the fruits of His Spirit among men."
—WILLIAM PENN.

"NOT fighting but suffering," says William Penn, "is a testimony peculiar to this people, . . . nor ought they for this to be obnoxious to civil government since if they cannot fight for it neither can they fight against it."[2] Their attitude was, "We will act justly, even generously

[1] Richard B. Gregg. *The Power of Non-violence,* pp. 205 and 178. Routledge, London, 1936.
[2] Sharpless. *A Quaker Experiment in Government,* p. 186.

with all, red men and white men alike. We will never be the aggressor. If attacked, therefore, we will always be in the right. We will not yield one iota of our rights willingly but will defend them by all means which in themselves are right. We cannot fight, for we believe that fighting itself is immoral and we *will not do wrong even for a righteous cause*.[1] If there is no other alternative we can suffer as we have shown our capacity to suffer in England and conquer by suffering."[2] They refused to admit an enemy but, having done their utmost duty, they trusted implicitly in Providence to protect them. 'Sufficient is Thine arm alone!'

The Quakers of this period believed with white-heat intensity "that they had . . . re-discovered a . . . spiritual Principle, which they thought was destined to revolutionise life, society, civil government, and religion. The Principle . . . was the presence of a Divine Light in man, a radiance from the central Light of the whole universe, penetrating the deeps of every soul, which if responded to, obeyed and accepted, is a guiding star, which would lead unto all truth . . . and put the Kingdom of God into actual operation here in the world."[3] Man is an imperfect instrument for the working out of a spiritual ideal, and many efforts made individually and collectively did not bring the expected results, nor appear as true as they were intentioned to be. Men of the highest integrity could and did make mistakes, but they strove to bring their standard within the realm of government and filled the Assembly with men, plain and just and true. As

[1] My italics.
[2] Ib. "Quakers in Pennsylvania," p. 469 in R. M. Jones' *Quakers in the American Colonies*. London, 1911.
[3] Sharpless. Op. cit., "Quakers in Pennsylvania," p. xvii.

long as this policy of justice with peace prevailed so did prosperity bless their land. To its founder the wealth of the Colony exceeded his wildest dreams, but only to be valued as making "happy homes and beneficent institutions," for in no way could worldly well-being supersede "spiritual righteousness, piety, beneficence: these were fruits for which the growth of riches was worth while and without which liberty itself would be no blessing."[1]

The first thirty years of the established colony of Pennsylvania were impregnated with difficulties and grievances, petty differences in opinion in the Assembly, disturbances through officious Governors, and some trouble with pirates and privateers. Then followed thirty years of settled, steady government, with peaceful conditions internally, prosperous trade relations, and a creditable money standard. The Indians were friendly, no military element existed, taxation was easy, no war was found necessary, politicians ruled with integrity and dignity. "Not a ripple of discontent"[2] stirred the calm waters of a serene, free, and progressive State. This 'Golden Age,' as Clarkson has called it, was the direct result of its being at liberty—given to it by the owner and ultimate controller, and this biographer adds: "How awful does the contemplation of it render the situation of statesmen, . . . if having within themselves the power of disseminating so much happiness, they have failed or neglected to dispense it! But still more awful, if, by wars, persecutions and other unjust proceedings, they have been the authors of unnecessary sufferings at home, or of misery to those aliens with

[1] Ib. Op. cit., p. 470.
[2] See Hirst. Op. cit., p. 370.

whom circumstances have unhappily led them to be concerned!"[1]

Negro slavery was an accepted custom in Pennsylvania when Penn took possession of it. This was a deplorable system and caused the true Quaker to be much exercised in his mind as to how to treat these men with the regard due to 'brothers in the Lord.' Very soon after his settlement there Penn introduced a motion to the Philadelphia Monthly Meeting, deprecating such methods of employment and desiring that attention be given to the well-being of the slaves, that "Friends . . . be careful in discharging a good conscience towards them in all respects, but more especially for the good of their souls."[2] Monthly Services were arranged for the negroes' instruction, and masters were requested to give every facility for their slaves to worship at Meetings. Further attempts to improve conditions for them were made by the introduction of bills to regulate their morality, their trials and punishments; but these were rejected till the negroes were better instructed. In a will dated 1701 Penn gives "my blacks their freedom,"[3] showing how strongly he felt in the matter. But Pastorius, whose sensitive mind had realised the enormity of the offence as early as 1688, could not succeed in getting its abolition considered. Much as the Quakers felt that "buying, selling and holding men in bondage was contrary to 'the first law of Christ,'"[4] yet they forbore from insisting on what appeared to them impossible. In 1712 they passed a Bill in Assembly levying a heavy tax on all imported

[1] Clarkson. Op. cit., p. 367.
[2] W. J. Buck. *William Penn in America*. Philadelphia, 1888 (p. 248).
[3] Ib., p. 249.   [4] Stoughton. Op. cit., p. 305.

Indians and negroes, but this was not accepted by the Home Government which considered the 'market-for-men' a profitable source of income for British traders! It was not till many years later that this despicable practice was abolished by law.

Emigrants continued to pour into this 'State without an army,' the population growing beyond all precedent, from 26,000 in 1701 to 60,000 in 1714, thence to 90,000 in 1718, to 280,000 in 1761 and 360,000 in 1776. The author of a publication—*The importance of the British plantations to these kingdoms, etc., considered* (London, printed 1731) states: "That Pennsylvania (which has not any particular staple like Carolina, Virginia and Maryland) and was begun to be planted so late as 1680, should at present have more white inhabitants in it than all Virginia, Maryland and both the Carolinas, is remarkable."[1]   Its trade leapt to almost fantastic figures in exports and imports; its wealth exceeded all other colonies in America. This influx of non-Quakers, the rush of commerce and the stupendous riches beyond anything they had ever known, combined to undermine the religious status of the Colony, and ultimately so overwhelmed the peace-loving, spiritual and modest Friends, as to break down their system, deprive them of their power of government, and make of Pennsylvania a worldly, competitive, commercialised State.

The system of education adopted was not at all satisfactory in building up a people ready to cope with the question of the material world.   Schools were not free, but Friends rendered mutual aid in these as in other matters.   Gradually their religion, narrowing

[1] Proud. Op. cit., vol. ii, p. 203.

itself with the necessary restrictions imposed by the practices of the less seriously-minded inhabitants, extended its cramping influence to the more secular side of life. No music or art found a place with them, and very soon Quakerism developed into an 'end-in-itself,' shrinking from contacts and thus getting crowded out by the social activities of the State. No such colleges as Harvard and Yale (Puritan) were established; education for them lacked the fearlessness their Principle called for. George Fox realised the urgency of training Friends in 'everything that is saving and useful in creation.'[1] Their neglect to found such institutions, which would have developed the individual outlook and increased wisdom by sharing experiences with more fully cultured intellects, seems one of the greatest causes of their failure "to win the commanding place in American civilisation of which their early history gave promise."[2]

At William Penn's death Hannah continued to direct affairs according to his wishes. As sole executrix of what was now an immensely valuable estate, she held a position of trust and great responsibility with benevolent dignity and capability during her life-time. Her three sons succeeded her as joint Proprietors, John, the eldest, having the prior claim to the property. James Logan had been a valued secretary to William Penn and acted as adviser to the successors, using his every power to forward the cause he knew to be so dear to the Founder of the Colony, especially with the Indians who respected and loved him. William Keith held the Governorship for Hannah from 1717 to 1726, when

[1] Sharpless. Op. cit., p. xxviii.
[2] Ib., p. xxvi.

he was superseded by Patrick Gordon, a really popular man, whose administration marked a period of harmonious activities and social well-being in the history of Pennsylvania. But one unhappy incident led to the estrangement of the Indians and eventually ended the Quaker peace policy. In 1732 Thomas Penn visited his territory and was joined by John in 1734. The former was not a desirable man at all: he was "unscrupulous, overbearing and dishonest . . . greedy, stingy and cruel"; nothing of his father's "goodness of heart or breadth of character"[1] had stamped a trace upon him. When the elder Penn had needed extra land for settlement he had made a 'walking survey' in accordance with native custom. Indians accompanied him, and the scheme was carried through leisurely and pleasantly, the distance covered in a given time was then allotted as the 'purchase area.' But the crafty son, when he required more land hired a sprinter, who walked further and therefore claimed a bigger area than could have been done honestly. The idea was a trick, and the plan a ruse to get property from the innocent Indians. They bitterly resented it, but as they could do nothing to retailiate, the episode rankled continuously and thence began petty warfares which ended in disaster. The return of the Proprietaries to England in 1736 and 1741 respectively, was welcomed rather than regretted in America.

George Thomas, a loyal Britisher, succeeded to the Governorship in 1738 and held office till 1748 when he was replaced by James Hamilton, of 'American birth and breeding."[2] Colonel Robert Hunter Morris

[1] Buell. Op. cit., p. 348.
[2] Buell.

was not so fortunate nor so popular. He took office in 1754 when fresh quarrels between England and Europe were stirring people to warlike activities in all parts of the Empire. Morris was a Puritan and a fighter, quite unsuited to rule peaceful Quakers, particularly so at this time when ill-feeling was being generated by such events as the defeat of Braddock, English officer of the Crown, who, attempting to take Fort Duquesne, failed, and was mortally wounded, his whole army unit being cut to pieces by French and Indians. The Assembly was a source of trouble and annoyance to this militant loyalist—they baulked his schemes of warfare at every turn. Persistently and efficaciously they refused to assign him money for such purposes. Within their memory lived the experience of having supplied Governor George Thomas with £4,000, "for bread, flour, wheat or other grain,"[1] the 'other grain' being skilfully interpreted to mean gunpowder, which took a very considerable portion of the grant. After many vain efforts to induce them to "adopt a vigorous and manly policy in the general system of defence"[2] he declared that "no man of honour, patriotism, or courage could act in concert with"[3] such a body, and so resigned (1756).

William Denny was the next authority to attempt to get some satisfactory working connection between the English sovereign, who wanted to extend an Empire, and the Quaker Assembly who wanted to live and serve God. To the latter the struggles and warrings in America were mere petty squabbles between the various nations for property and prestige, neither justifiable

[1] Sharpless. *A Quaker Experiment in Government*, p. 211.
[2] Buell. Op. cit., p. 353.
[3] Ib., do.

nor righteous—to the former the matter was the just and right cause of building a British Empire. The time had to come, however, when the Friends' influence was no longer powerful enough to withstand the pressure of demands for war. During the 74 years of the life of Pennsylvania, Quakers had maintained a working majority in the Assembly, even when they were only one-seventh of the population. Pennsylvanians still voted them into power. But little by little their authority weakened, and they realised that the only way to preserve the Constitution as established by the Charter, was to allow the popular war party to take their places: they had to sacrifice power or principle!

The culminating scene of 'The Holy Experiment' was enacted by the Quakers themselves in the meeting of Assembly in 1756. So militant a spirit prevailed that the Governor and Council persuaded the Assembly to accept their declaration of war on the Delaware Indians. This was too much! With the banner of their faith still unfurled, those men who knew the Inner peace of the Kingdom of God and His Righteousness, left the concourse. They walked out; but their testimony lives —a substantial, holy precedent for posterity.

Chapter VIII

THE PENNSYLVANIAN EXPERIMENT—
A VIEW FROM WITHIN

(a)

Two pamphlets, both issued in the year 1755 provide, as it were, a glimpse of the final stages of the Pennsylvanian Experiment immediately before it was irrevocably abandoned. In them the whole question of defence, and of the difficulties which were constantly arising between the Assembly and the Governors are discussed, and light is thrown upon the causes, external and internal, which brought to an end Penn's scheme of government as he had conceived it.

The pamphlet[1] is assumed to be the work of a certain William Smith, D.D.[2] who is designated by the author of the second pamphlet as one of 'the Governor's men,' and who closes his brief Statement with the threat to leave the country and "leave his bones" in the land of

---

[1] *A brief State of the Province of Pennsylvania in which the Conduct of their Assemblies for several Years past is impartially examined, and the true Cause of the continual Encroachments of the French displayed, more especially the secret Design of their late unwarrantable Invasion and Settlement upon the River Ohio.*

To which is annexed An easy Plan for restoring Quiet in the public Measures of that Province, and defeating the ambitious Views of the French in time to come.

In a Letter from a Gentleman who has resided many years in Pennsylvania to his Friend in London. The Second Edition. London. Printed for R. Griffiths at the Dunciad, in Paternoster Row. 1755.

[2] William Cushing. *Anonyms. A Dictionary of Revealed Authorship.* 1890 (vol. i).

his birth, presumably Britain. The word 'person' is spelt 'parson' in a contemporary letter.

In the second pamphlet[1] the charges made in the first are taken up and dealt with, and an attempt is made to explain and justify the action of the Assembly and the attitude of others in the province.

The 'Gentleman' admits that, "of all the British Colonies in North America, Pennsylvania is the most flourishing" (*A brief State*, p. 4). But he asks why the Assemblies are against defending the country, and why "the several Sums" offered for the King's use have not been accepted (op. cit., p. 14). To the second question it is replied that "the assembly of Pennsylvania have always been as forward to contribute, upon any emergency, as any of the other colonies." The case is cited of a grant of £20,000 in 1754 for the King's use made to Governor Morris, in a message to whom it was stated that "we account it our duty to do everything in our power to comply with his Majesty's royal orders" (*Answer*, p. 4). It is further declared that "they [the Assembly] are not against the defence of their country by military methods, but that they, not only in their frequent messages to the Governor declare their readiness to provide for the defence of the colony, but even ordered £5,000 to be laid out for purchasing fresh victuals, and such other necessaries as they should think expedient for the use of the King's troops at their arrival" (*Pennsylvanian Gazette*, January 14th, 1755).

[1] *An ANSWER To an invidious Pamphlet entitled A Brief State, etc., Wherein are exposed The many false assertions of the Author or Authors of the said pamphlet, with a view to render the Quakers of Pennsylvania and their Government obnoxious to the British Parliament and Ministry. And the Several Transactions, most grossly misrepresented therein, set in their true light. London: Printed for S. Bladon, in Paternoster Row. MDCCLV.*

In reply to the second question the reason given is that
the Governors had been trying "under various pretences
to get 'the disposal of the public money into their
hands, without being obliged to give an account to the
Assembly.'"

The matter appears to have been further complicated
by a bill which became law on May 12th, 1740. In
1739 the Assembly had "applied to Governor Thomas
. . . to pass a bill for establishing a fund of £80,000
in paper money for the convenience of the province."
The lords justices of England sent Thomas an instruction issued under "an act of the 6th of Queen Ann"
requiring him or the commander-in-chief *for the time
being*, not to pass any act whereby bills of credit should
be issued in lieu of money without a clause to suspend
the execution of it till the pleasure of the Crown should
be known" (*Pennsylvanian Gazette*, December 26th.
Assembly Message, December 20th). But Governor
Thomas considered "that the crown had by charter
granted *full powers to the people for passing all laws whatever*
they should judge fit for the benefit of the colony"; and
that the paper currency was necessary. He therefore
gave his consent to the bill which was *recommended to the
Crown by the board of trade* and received the Royal
Sanction. In 1746 Thomas gave his assent to another
bill granting £5,000 for the King's use, to be sunk on
the excise in ten years without a suspending clause, this
precedent being followed subsequently by Governor
Hamilton. Yet the suspending clause (no longer
applicable to Pennsylvania) appears to have been made
a convenient excuse by Governors for not accepting
the grants voted by the Assembly. Their grievance (as
alleged in the *Answer*, p. 9) was that they could not

have "as exorbitant salaries as they might demand."

The charges relating to inadequate measures of defence are next considered. The writer of the *Answer* states "that from New York all the way to South Carolina there are no fortifications along the coasts; so that the Pennsylvanians in this respect are not more blameable than their Southern neighbours." He admits that Philadelphia lies 150 miles from the sea, and that the river is of very difficult navigation, especially for vessels of 200 or 300 tons . . . so that in effect this is the part of the whole province, with respect to which least danger is to be apprehended. He even goes so far as to declare that forts ought to be built all along their coasts, as well as borders, in the places most exposed to the invasion of an enemy, either by sea or land.[1] To the suggestion of the 'Gentleman' "that the French will take possession of the whole province," the answer is made that the French with but three forts could hardly be said to have "a stronger footing" in the province than the inhabitants "possessed of the body of it" to the confessed number of 220,000 (p. 25). No, the Quakers who are accused of being so tenacious of their rights do not (it is stated) intend to part with either their country or their privileges to the French (op. cit., p. 27). They are satisfied that it is not in so great danger as the Governor's party would make them believe; they cannot accept the story of 6,000 French from Quebec being magically transported to the Ohio "without being seen or heard by any body" (op. cit., p. 28).

[1] This seems a strange admission for one who had previously stated that, among the Quakers, it was "a point of conscience not to bear arms" (p. 15), but it must be remembered that at this time Friends in Pennsylvania were not unanimous on the question of defence.

The next matter to be taken up relates to the Militia Bill. It is maintained in the *Answer* (p. 32) "that if a militia law was to be established in Pennsylvania unless it was managed better than it is in other provinces this colony had better be without it. . . . Does the Governor expect that the assembly will of their own accord propose a bill of that kind? why does not the Governor 'get the attorney-general to draw one up in a proper manner suitable to the principles of the people whom they are to apply to, and see if the assembly will not accept it?" (op. cit., p. 32). The writer points out that Quakers, though they are, as a result of religious scruples, averse to bear arms themselves, and are unwilling to fight in person, yet "are ready to pay those who will . . . and that Pennsylvania will afford men enough willing to fight, without compelling the Quakers, appears from the proprietary instructions to the Governor, requiring men to be raised, but yet so far as not to oblige any to bear arms who may be conscientiously scrupulous" (op. cit., p. 60).

Finally, an accusation has to be met with regard to the German settlers in Pennsylvania. "By what means," enquires the author of the *Brief State*, "do the Quakers, who are so small a Part of the Inhabitants, and whose measures are so unpopular, get continually chosen into our assemblies?" (op. cit., p. 26). In response to his own query he maintains that the Quakers had (as modern speech would phrase it) indulged in a deliberate and subversive course of propaganda among the Germans through the services of a printer named Saüer. Through his means his countrymen had been told that "there was a design to enslave them, to force their young men to be soldiers . . . that a military

Law was to be made, insupportable taxes to be laid upon them, and in a Word, that all the Miseries they suffered in Germany with heavy aggravations would be their Lot, unless they joined to keep in the Quakers" (op. cit., p. 27). In consequence of this, the Germans who had hitherto continued peaceful, without meddling in elections, came down in crowds and carried all before them.

What was the reply to all these accusations of Quaker mal-practices? They stated that "the land is properly their birthright, and the possession in justice belongs to them. They cannot therefore be blamed for using their endeavours to keep possession, and hinder others from reaping the fruit of their labours, after taking so much care to bring the Province into its present flourishing condition. Prudence, therefore, as well as justice, evinces the obligation and even necessity, of returning the Quakers in the assembly" (*Answer*, p. 66). Allusion is made to the election of 1744 "when privateer sailors in the harbour of Philadelphia, under the influence of the Governor's men came armed to the Court House, where the Sheriff was then taking the pole, and with open violence hindered the legal voters, who were in the interests of the Quakers, from voting: knocking down and beating in the most barbarous manner all who appeared not to be of their party. The Governor subsequently granted *noli prosequi's*" (op. cit., p. 67). And the question is asked: "Is it then to be wondered after this, if ever since they call in the Germans to their aid?" It is stated that to these Germans "is, in a great measure, to be ascribed the present flourishing condition of the province, owing to their industry in cultivating the lands, and the wealth

G—D

which they brought with them into Pennsylvania."
Ridicule is cast upon the over-estimated power of the
German printer who is termed "this Herculean typo-
grapher." He is said to have been "a useful member
in the society . . . in preserving the liberty of the
subject, by communicating and exposing the evil
designs and oppressions of the Governors to the people
. . . a proof of public spirit which an English printer
at Philadelphia had not the courage or zeal to give"
(op. cit., p. 70). In refuting the charge that "the
Germans had grown insolent, sullen, and turbulent,
in some counties threatening the lives of all who oppose
their views" (*State*, p. 28) it is suggested that "surely
such sons of slaughter cannot be averse to arms!"
(*Answer*, p. 70).

The conclusions reached by the 'Gentleman' who
claims that "truth and duty obliged him to take up the
pen" are five in number:

"1. To oblige all those who sit in Assembly to take the
Oaths of Allegiance to his Majesty, and perhaps
a Test or Declaration that they will not refuse to
defend their Country against all his Majesty's
Enemies.

2. To suspend the Right of Voting for Members of
Assembly from the Germans, till they have a
sufficient Knowledge of our Language and Constitution.

3. To encourage Protestant Ministers and School-
masters among them.

4. To induce the Germans to learn English.

5. That no News-Papers, Almanacks, or any other

periodical Paper . . . be printed or circulated in a foreign Language" (*State*, pp. 40-42).

To these conclusions it is stated in the *Answer* that "the first is calculated not only to exclude the Quakers wholly from the Assembly by obliging them to take an oath, but also to compel them personally to take up arms against their consciences. The second to deprive three fourths of the people of either the privilege of sitting in the Assembly or voting is considered to be 'not reasonable at all' " (*Answer*, p. 77). The three remaining articles are found to be in effect contained in the second (Op. cit., p. 78).

The anomaly of the whole position may be summed up in the words of the writer of the *Answer*: "After all the having proprietary Governments in a country is incompatible with the rights of Crowns. It is a kind of *imperium in imperio*, and consequently a solecism in politics" (*Answer*, p. 54).

In 1755 the Pennsylvanian Experiment was struggling against external difficulties, some of which appear to have been almost, if not quite, insuperable. Dependence upon the approval of a monarchical system across the ocean, subject to the demands of governors who might be oppressive, self-seeking, or military-minded, and who were themselves attempting an impossible task in an impossible situation, exposed to a lack of sympathy from certain elements of the population and to the open and avowed hostility of others, like the Scottish-Irish; existing in the midst of supposedly unfriendly peoples like the frustrated French and the disappointed and disillusioned Indians, the Quaker minority in the province found itself seriously hampered in its efforts to uphold the principles on which the State had originally been founded. Yet it can hardly be maintained with truth and justice that the Experiment was wrecked solely by opposing forces from without. It must surely be acknowledged that shattering and disruptive forces had been also working from within.

The Friends of 1755 were not those of the first years of the century. They had not the unwavering faith and unbending convictions of Claypole and Richard Hill. A spirit of distrust seems to have made itself felt; distrust of others and especially distrust of themselves, and of their ability to hold fast to their testimony as 'absolutists' in the face of threatening dangers. They seem to have doubted if that testimony could be kept 'pure and undefiled.' Under the original scheme of its Founder, Pennsylvania was to have no defence organisation whatever—no forts, no armed men. The Holy Experiment was to be a new way of life in a New World. But when (as the author of the *Answer to the brief State* admits) the Quakers could envisage the erection of a single fort or could contemplate the idea of some one else fighting for them[1] the 'holiness' of the Experiment was at an end. If one fort, why not one hundred? If the use of material weapons was to be adopted for the protection of property, or against rival Empire-builders was to be thought necessary, and countenanced, then the methods of the old world must

[1] In the *Answer* the case is reported of Mr. Hull, a Quaker of Rhode Island, who commanded a vessel of which he was owner. While at sea a French privateer, coming up with him, the captain ordered him to strike. The Quaker replied that he would neither surrender his property nor fight for it, but would enquire if a non-Quaker aboard "was inclined to fight." A man called Charles "accepted the encounter; and falling to work with the Frenchman, soon obliged him to sheer off." Mr. Hull's account of this incident when reported in London led to the promotion of Charles to the rank of Sir Charles Wager." (Op. cit., p. 61.)

be revived in the new. If *one* potential 'enemy' be admitted, the earth is full of them and defence becomes a necessity. Fear rules. Inasmuch and in so far as the Pennsylvanian Friends felt compelled by outward circumstances to yield one iota of their witness, they were themselves responsible for the crumbling of the imperfect structure. But the Experiment *has demonstrated for all time that* for a brief space *unarmed security was actually attained* by a small human community whilst it remained *true to the essential principles* on which such security must rest.

(b)

The author of *A brief State* subsequently added a sequel to his former pamphlet.[1] In this the same charges against the Assembly are repeated, letters from certain irate individuals are quoted, and it is even suggested that the whole scheme of the Quaker refusal to bear arms was a French plot contrived by "a faithful Jesuit." It was said that this man was "sent to England to found a Sect of *Quietists* or *Non-resistants* who held it unworthy to spill Christian blood, and if you smote them on the one Cheek would turn the other also." It was hoped that "this Sect would multiply exceedingly," and in that case "le grand Monarque would have made an easy conquest of the whole island of Britain" (p. 16).

This seemingly fantastic idea is followed by the accusation that "we have not, as a Province, *armed* a single Man" and that Braddock had been left without

---

[1] *A Second Letter to a friend in London written by the same Gentleman is entitled "A brief View of the Conduct of Pennsylvania For the Year 1755," being a Sequel to his former pamphlet.* London, 1756.

support. The Assembly had refused to provide at the
request of Governor Hamilton the waggons, horses etc.,
for military purposes, the Quakers saying that they
would rather suffer than pay towards such Purposes
(p. 30). They likewise refused to grant lands to
Colonels, Majors, Captains, Lieutenants, Ensigns, and
common soldiers west of the Alleghany Mountains.
Then follows an account of Indian raids and nameless
atrocities, and the subsequent petitions made by Colonel
Weiser, the Provincial Interpreter and two other Indian
chiefs. The Indian spokesman, Scarroyady, addressed
the Governor and Assembly and desired, as was the
usual request, authority to have recourse to "the
Hatchet" and for a Militia Law. The so-called "Back
Inhabitants," and particularly the Scottish-Irish were
greatly incensed against the Assembly, but its position
was much strengthened by the visit of three Quaker
preachers who arrived from England—one male and
the other two females. The latter urged and exhorted
members of the Assembly to continue faithful to that
distinguishing tenet of their religion, which restrained
them from bearing arms, or contributing to defence.
The Quaker Meeting itself delivered on November 6th,
1755 an Address to the Representatives of the Freemen
of the Province in General Assembly met. In this
admonition a warning was given against raising sums
of money and putting them into the hands of Com-
mittees who might apply them to purposes inconsistent
with the "PEACABLE TESTIMONY we profess, and
have borne to the world" and the danger of so doing
was stressed as "destructive or our *religious* Liberties
affecting the *fundamental Part of our Constitution* and the
enjoyment of Liberty of Conscience" (pp. 62, 63).

Members of the Assembly appear to have reasoned that neither French nor Indians will hurt the Quakers, and if the border colonists insist on war-like and provocative measures they must not be surprised at similar action being taken against themselves. An appeal for the defence of "bleeding Fellow-subjects" was made by several of the principal inhabitants of Philadelphia on November 12th, and a remonstrance by the Mayor (William Plumstead), Aldermen and Common-council of the City was lodged on November 24th. As a concession to these demands "a sort of Military-bill" was framed entitled "An Act for the better ordering and regulating such as are *willing* and *desirous* to be united for Military Purposes within this Province." This bill made it lawful for Freemen of the Province to form themselves into companies and choose their officers to be approved by the Governor. This measure was the first of its kind, being an actual Militia Act, as opposed to the method previously adopted of the enrollment of volunteers. Regiments of such had been formed as early as the winter of 1748, and had been called Association Regiments. There had been thirteen companies in Philadelphia and one hundred companies in all. At this time the spirit and influence of the Friends' Meetings was such that public legislative sanction could not be given to such warlike proceedings, thus showing that the majority of the Quakers were still ready to depend upon "the arm of the Lord" and the "Great Watcher of Israel."[1] But the struggle to rely solely on spiritual weapons had been a long and severe one. As far back as 1710 James

[1] John Fannings Watson. *Annals of Philadelphia and Pennsylvania in the olden time.* Philadelphia, 1844 (vol. i, pp. 500-506).

Logan had stated that the clamours and abuses from such men (the hot church party) of the Friends in government tires them and makes them weary of the burden. When the Queen had asked for a quota for Canada, Friends knew not how to act or how to refuse, seeing that all the other colonies had contributed more than was required. Isaac Norris also declared that "these of the church grew very uneasy and unneighbourly in their expressions because of the defenceless situation of the place. They are for a coercive law, that all may be obliged to bear arms, or else they will do nothing." James Logan was never averse to measures of protection, that is, for a defensive war. John Churchman, who was known as 'the public Friend,' felt himself called to express his disapprobation of such public callings generally as too exposing in their tendency for tender minds. When it is remembered that John Churchman saw the bodies of a German, his wife and son in a waggon in Philadelphia after they had been killed and scalped by the Indians, and brought into the city (on the occasion of a gathering of the Quakers) for the purpose of inciting the people to unite in preparation for war on the Indians, a certain measure of sympathy may be felt for his attitude of mind. A warning voice calling itself 'The Watchman' in the *Pennsylvanian Journal* delivered a similar call to return to first principles. It said: "From the moment we Friends began to lose sight of our original institution we erred greatly. Let us return to our original plan and leave the concerns of this world entirely to the men of this world."

Some of the Quakers residing in the city of Philadelphia on behalf of themselves and many others, addressed themselves to the representatives of the freemen of the Province in General Assembly met. In their address they referred to the wise, worthy, first Proprietary and called to mind in particular his emphatic and prophetic words which were as follows: "If Friends here keep to God, and in the justice, mercy, equity and fear of the Lord, their enemies will be their footstool; if not, their heirs and my heirs too will loose all, and desolation will follow."[1]

The Militia Act of 1755 did not satisfy those (like the writer of the *Brief View*) who maintained that defence and enrolment in a militia was the duty of all. These declared unequivocally that the Quakers, as such, were unfit to be "Rulers, Assembly-Men, Politicians and Monopolizers of Power" (op. cit., p. 85). The Assembly-Men replied that their policy had brought Pennsylvania to its acknowledged condition of unexampled prosperity, but in the face of the ever-growing popular insistence on a change of method, did not feel themselves justified in retaining their control of the Assembly. They withdrew when war was demanded, and four years later, in 1759, four Quakers (by name Mahlon Kirkbride, William Hoge, Peter Dicks and Nathaniel Pennock) vacated their seats in the Assembly at the request of the Council of the Crown in London, because it was a time of war.[2]

[1] Hazard's *Register*, vol. viii, p. 274.
[2] Watson. Op. cit., vol. i, p. 506.

(c)

The year which saw the last of the Quakers in the Assembly of Pennsylvania, saw also the issue of yet a third pamphlet[1] which claims the merit of impartiality in a vexed and bitter controversy. Its main object appears to have been "to demonstrate by incontestable Vouchers, that ARBITRARY Proprietary Instructions have been the *true* and *only* cause of the refusal of supplies and the late defenceless state of the province." It is dedicated to William Pitt, one of His Majesty's principal Secretaries of State. The pamphlet called *A brief State* is said to be the result of baffled malice, and the rage of a disappointed party, whose *evident design* is to sap the foundation of the Constitution. The writer of *An Impartial view* maintains that by Penn's Charter the Assembly is authorised to grant supplies *in their own way*, and that the private interest of a Ruler is to be subservient to the good of the people whom he rules. The office and function of the Governor must coincide and co-operate with the public utility. But in this particular instance the interests of the Governor are dependent upon the good will and pleasure of certain individuals who, as in the case of Governor Morris, issue private instructions inconsistent with the liberty of the people. It is shown that the Assembly, time after time, offered the supplies requested, or demanded, by the Home Government upon certain conditions, or accompanied by suggestions as to the raising of the required sums, but that the Governor

---

[1] *A True and Impartial State of the Province of Pennsylvania. The whole being a full Answer to the Pamphlets entitled A Brief View and a Brief State. Philadelphia. Printed by W. W. Dunlap at the Newest Printing Office. MDCCLIX.* (This work is attributed to Benjamin Franklin by Cushing.)

rejected these, either on the grounds of the suspension clause, or because he wished to deprive the Assembly of its established powers and privileges. The conditions or proposals were found to be unacceptable, ostensibly to the Governor, but very possibly to the Proprietaries. It is also shown that the clause known as the 'suspension clause' became no longer applicable to the southern counties as soon as the authorities of the Home Government had had sufficient opportunity to examine, and to satisfy themselves, with regard to the currencies of the American legislatures. Finally, it is declared that when at length the Assembly framed a Militia law it was refused by the Governor, who without even suggesting an amendment, sought to stir up public opinion in favour of the old method of Association. Proprietary instructions are declared to be the cause of such an entirely unsatisfactory state of affairs, and a desire to safeguard the pockets, as well as the liberties of the people, rather than an unwillingness to perform their duties, is claimed to lie at the root of the motives and actions of the Assembly.

The thesis thus put forward by the author of *A True and Impartial State*, later revealed to be Benjamin Franklin, receives further support in his *Historical Review of Pennsylvania* in which he discusses in detail the various difficulties of the situation.[1] Here it is said that the Assemblies of that province have acted from the beginning "on the *defensive* only. The defensive is what every man, by the right and law of nature is intitled to . . . Penn, the founder of the Colony, founded it

---

[1] *An Historical Review of Pennsylvania from its origin so far as regards the several points of controversy, which have from time to time arisen between the several Governments of the province and their several Assemblies. Founded on authentic documents.* 1759.

upon Magna Charta: and, as we have seen, the Birth-
rights of his Followers were rather enlarged than dimin-
ished by his Institutions. . . . It is as apparent, on the
other hand, That these Proprietaries have acted an
offensive Part; have set up unwarrantable claims; have
adhered to them by Instructions yet more unwarrantable; have availed themselves of the Dangers and
Distresses of the Province, and made it their Business
(at least their Deputies have) to increase the Terrors
of the times, purposely to unhinge the present system;
and by the Dint of Assumptions, Snares, Menaces,
Aspersions, Tumults, and every other unfair Practice
whatsoever, would have either bullied or wheedled
the Inhabitants out of the privileges they were born
to . . . and This being the Truth, the plain Truth,
and nothing but the Truth, there is no need to direct
the Censures of the Public" (p. 379).

(d)

In the year 1755, another pamphlet[1] appeared, which
supplies contemporary evidence of French and British
rivalry in America. In this pamphlet it is stated that
the French "are still much inferior to the English in
numbers. They know this defect on their own side
perfectly well, but depend for their success upon what
they know to be more advantageous than a superiority
in numbers, and that is, the division which reigns
among the colonies, their defenceless state, and slowness
in action" (p. 3). It is also maintained that although
Louis XIV had in the year 1686 entered into a treaty

---

[1] *State of the British and French Colonies in North America in two letters to
a Friend.* London. Printed for A. Millar in the Strand. MDCCLV.

of neutrality with England for North America, he had in 1688 embarked upon a project to subdue the British colonies in that part of the continent, and had begun with the attempt to conquer the State of New York. As the result of an exact enquiry the whole population of French Canada had been estimated in 1754 to number 45,000 persons, of whom 15,000 were capable of bearing arms. The French themselves are said to have recorded an armed force of 18,000, but this statement was disputed in favour of a smaller figure, namely, 12,000. The policy of the English colonists, according to the author of the pamphlet was "to *out-fort*, as well as *out-settle* them." In the second letter the writer says of Pennsylvania with regard to the question of population there was no poll tax, and no militia roll by which to compute (p. 135).

The history of the dispute called by the author of the *Brief State* "the secret design of the French" and their settlement in the Ohio country is given as follows. The land in question formed part of the territory originally granted to Virginia, and many Virginians were tempted into it by the fertility of the soil and the friendly spirit of the Indians. Meantime the French had, in 1699, made a settlement at the mouth of the Mississippi and opened up communications in the country by means of the River Illinois. They began to build forts along the Mississippi and to enter, by degrees, into Ohio. They erected a fort at the mouth of the river. In 1749 a grant was obtained of 600,000 acres in the same country, to certain merchants and others, of Virginia and London, to trade under the name of the Ohio Company. In 1750 the French complained that the Twigtwees (Miami) had encroached on

French territory by trading with Indians who were friendly to themselves. This was the beginning of French and Colonial rivalry. When the English-speaking settlers began to construct a fort in the forks' 'of the Ohio' (the word Ohio or Hohîo is said to mean 'Fair River') the French took possession of it before it could be completed. The French drove away the English, and completed the fort for themselves. The Seven Years' War was the immediate consequence.[1] The next trouble was with the Indians. They objected to the use and disposal of their lands by Pennsylvanians, Virginians, and others, who acted clandestinely and "without any title, either by right or purchase." It is acknowledged in the pamphlet that when a certain Mr. Gist (or Ghist) had made a survey in 1751 he had been very careful to conceal his design from the Indians. The result of such a policy had been that the Ohio Indians preferred to ally themselves with the French, who *openly* averred their intention to establish themselves in the country. The author of the *State* asserts "that the Indians gave no consent either to the grant of the land nor to the building of the fort," although the Pennsylvanian Assembly was informed, falsely, that such consent had been forthcoming. The erection of the fort aroused suspicion in the minds of the Indians against the Pennsylvanian traders and the direct outcome of this proceeding was the transference of Indian allegiance to the French. The author's comments on the result are as follows: "It would be better to purchase gradually all Indian settlements by agreement, to buy their friendship, tho' dear, than to lose their assistance."

The gaps in the above narrative may be filled in by

[1] Encyc. Brit., XI. Ed., Ohio.

the account given by a writer of a much later date who deals with the history of the Ohio Company.[1] When the packmen of Pennsylvania and Virginia pushed bodily into the Ohio valley, the interests of Pennsylvania were advanced by the efforts of two brothers-in-law—George Croghan, who had been the British crown agent with the Indians, and Colonel Trent. They decided that the protection of trade required a fortification at the forks of the Ohio. In 1753 Governor Hamilton urged the necessity of having some places of strength and security built on the Ohio under the name of 'traders' or 'truck houses' which might serve as retreats to 'our Indians.' (Thus the fort mentioned in the pamphlet is later called a 'store-house.') When news of an approaching crisis reached the British Government, Sir Charles Holderness, the Secretary of State, at once instructed the Pennsylvanian authorities to use force, if necessary, to expel the French from the undoubted limits of his Majesty's dominions. The opinion of members of the Assembly appears to have been that "to advance the interests of the Ohio Company was not worth the risk of a harrowing border war" (op. cit., p. 307). By 1756, however, the Pennsylvanian Government, despite the view of the Quakers in the Assembly, established "a line of palisaded posts from the Delaware to the new road which had been opened to the mountains" (op. cit., p. 373).

[1] Justin Winsor. *The Mississippi Basin: The struggle in America between England and France.* 1697-1863. Houghton Mifflin, Boston. 1895.

THE END

Appendix I

THE PHILADELPHIA PRISON

(a)

In his account of a visit to the prison at Philadelphia, Turnbull[1] places on record his impressions generally and the features which particularly impressed him. These were the cleanliness of all parts—including the kitchens, sleeping apartments, etc., and the good quality of the food—*mush*, a nourishing grain, and bread, but very little meat. Another marked reform was the absence of irons and of all physical means of restraint, and the non-use of corporal punishment. In accordance with the Pennsylvanian legal code, certain of the prison buildings were equipped as workshops for various industries such as the manufacture of nails, shoemaking, sawing marble, and among the women, spinning and the making of garments. Turnbull remarks upon the selection and apparent fitness of the officials for their special duties, and turnkeys and others seemed to him to have adopted a helpful and friendly attitude towards their charges, who showed no sign of hatred or bitterness, but rather appreciation of the efforts to re-establish them as useful citizens.

[1] Robert J. Turnbull (of South Carolina). *A visit to the Philadelphia Prison.* Philadelphia, 1797.

The prison was self-supporting, labour being paid wages slightly lower than those outside, the money earned being appropriated in the first instance to the cost of feeding and housing the prisoners, then for restitution in the case of wrongs inflicted on others, and finally for the convicts' own subsequent use. Prison regulations were rigidly enforced, the penalty for infringement being solitary confinement in absolutely bare and comfortless cells. The idea was that this punishment would, as Turnbull asserts, give ample opportunity for reflection and resolution upon amendment of life. The period might be as short as forty-eight hours, and the theory was that the experience of solitude would quickly cause the offender to prefer, and consequently to seek, the ordered life of associated, if compulsory, work within the prison workshops. Such stringent measures hardly appear in keeping with "the wise and human administration adopted in every part" of which Turnbull writes in the title-page of his narrative. Prison existence was indeed an ordered life. Silence was maintained and divine worship insisted upon. Yet the absence of brutality (apart from the mental torture of solitary confinement) the division of the prison population into various classes—thus avoiding in many cases needless contamination and degradation—and the hope of release and restoration to society, appears to have worked well and instances of recidivism were few.

While he acknowledges "the gradual reformation and present improved state of the penal laws of Pennsylvania," Turnbull finds it necessary to make an earnest appeal for the abolition of the death penalty, even in the case of murder, for which crime alone capital punishment had been retained in the province. He declares that "crimes may be called diseases of the state, perpetrators of them the parts affected, legislators the prescribing physicians. How surprising that the only remedy should be the amputation of the infected limb!" He cannot believe that the security of a government or nation depends upon the existence of one poor delinquent, or that, since private revenge is a thing to be abhorred, the same should not be felt with regard to public executions. He avers that the punishment of death is an encroachment on the rights of the citizen and entirely un-Christian in principle and method. He states the three objects of penal laws to be the amendment of the criminal, reparation to the injured society or individual, and prevention of the same offence. He maintains that by the laws of Pennsylvania all the ends of punishment are achieved: restitution to injured society is produced by the personal industry and services of the convict; reformation is naturally effected from living a regular, sober, and moral life during his confinement, and the fact of the offender being brought to justice would always operate as a sufficient example.

After dealing fully with the inefficacy of a sanguinary code, Turnbull concludes with the reminder that every punishment which is not absolutely necessary for the prevention of crime is cruel, and a tyrannical act.

(b)

John Howard's record of his investigations with
regard to the conditions of gaols in Britain and on the
Continent enables the student of penal methods to
form some ideas of Penn's attempt to introduce a more
humane system in his new colony. Howard's account
is called *The State of the Prisons in England and of some
Foreign Prisons*, and it seems possible that some of the
reforms which were to be found in the prisons of
Pennsylvania had previously existed in Holland and
Germany. Penn visited these countries and may have
noticed and approved the methods of dealing with
prisoners in the places where he stayed. When Howard
made his tour of inspection more than a hundred years
later (in 1778, 1781 and 1783) he saw the Rasp-house
at Rotterdam where the men were chopping and
rasping logwood, combing, spinning and carding wool,
and a few making fishing-nets, and sorting coffee-
berries. The women were spinning wool and flax
(whence the alternative name of Spin-house) and
carding hair, or winding at a great wheel. They were
clean and apparently healthy and well. At Harlem
"Taylors were employed in the way of their profession"
and one person was working at a loom on flowered
damask, because that had been his former trade. At
Amsterdam Howard saw the old Rasp-house or Work-
house, and records that it was a well-regulated house
of industry. The produce of the prisoners' work was
applied to the maintenance of the house, and the
deficiency was made up from the Spin-house tax.
Want of pure air was the most disagreeable feature of

such places in general, and in many instances the offensive atmosphere resulted in unhealthy and diseased conditions, especially among the children in orphan-houses. Yet Howard's general conclusion was that in Dutch prisons the food was good, and the inmates employed in useful labour in clean and neat surroundings. He was also impressed by the humanity and attention of the magistrates and governors.

Very different was the state of affairs observed in England. There was indeed the same appalling lack of sweet, fresh air which Howard terms "the genuine cordial of life." The result of the shutting out of this life-giving cordial he describes as "Hell in miniature!" But there was also lack of food, lack of water, and lack of every kind of useful or beneficial employment. As a direct consequence of these deprivations the utmost misery held sway among the prison population, who were ravaged by gaol-fever and in some cases loaded with irons. Some prisons had no sewers, others no allowance of straw; men and women spent their time in "sloth, profaneness and debauchery." Howard's conclusion was expressed in his own words: "I am sure that a prison mends no mortals" (op. cit., p. 20).

Appendix II

THE FREE SOCIETY OF TRADERS

A folio pamphlet "printed in London for Benjamin Clark, in George Yard, in Lombard street, printer to the society of Pennsilvania 1682," is entitled *The articles, settlements and offices of the Free Society of Traders in Pennsilvania, agreed upon by divers merchants and others for the better improvement and government of trade in that province.*

In the Preface the Society is described as "A society without oppression: wherein all may be concerned that will: and yet have the same liberty of private traffique, as though there were no Society at all. . . . So that this Society is calculated both to promote the public good and to encourage the private. . . . For here a few hands do the work of the whole, and by this honest and free device, the whole will be furnished fresh and fresh from time to time in the nature of a Bank. This union of traffique prevents emulation: for everyone is interested in everyone's prosperity; and the profit must be greater and surer; and navigation, manufacture, and arts better improved than by force of private and divided stocks."

The Preface, signed Nicholas More, James Claypole and Philip Ford, ends with the assurance that "this Society is endowed with divers immunities and privileges, by grant and charter of William Penn, governor of that province."

Then follow twenty-nine Articles, the first of which lays it down that no one in England should have more than one vote whatever amount he might subscribe, unless he also possessed one thousand acres of land in Pennsilvania "with some inhabitants upon it."

Article III declares that "all that are inhabitants in Pennsilvania shall have for *two twenty-five pounds, one vote*: and each *fifty pounds* single *one vote*: *one hundred* pounds two votes: *three hundred* pounds, *three* votes, and none more" (Hazard's *Register*, June 21st, 1828, vol. i, pp. 394-397).

Appendix III

THE LAWS OF PENNSYLVANIA

In Hazard's *Register*, vol. i, p. 357 may be read the
forty Laws of Pennsylvania as agreed upon in England.
Some of these throw a certain light on social customs
and conditions of the time as well as on the penal
methods adopted. Law X enacts: That all prisons shall
be work-houses for felons, vagrants, and loose and idle
persons; whereof one shall be in every county. Law
XIII lays it down that all prisons shall be free as to
fees, food and lodging, while Law XVIII states that
all fines shall be moderate and saving men's contene-
ments, merchandize or wainage. Law XXXVIII
relates to manners and morals and reads as follows:
That as a careless and corrupt administration of Justice
draws the wrath of God upon magistrates, so the wild-
ness and looseness of the people provoke the indignation
of God against a country: Therefore that all offences
against God as swearing, cursing, lying, prophane
talking, drunkenness, drinking of healths, obscene words,
incest, sodomy, rape, whoredom, fornication and other
uncleanness (not to be repeated), all treasons, mis-
prisons, murders, duels, felony, sedition, maims, forcible
entries, and other violences of the persons and estates
of the inhabitants within this province: all prizes,
stage-plays, cards, dice, May games, gamesters, masques,
revels, bull-baitings, cock-fightings, and the like, which
excite the people to rudeness, cruelty, looseness and
irreligion, shall be respectively discouraged and

severely punished, according to the appointment of
the governor and freemen in provincial council and
general assembly; as also all proceedings contrary to
those laws, that are not here made expressly penal.

The imposition of a fine appears to have been a
penalty which was often imposed, though not always
exacted. It is recorded in Watson's *Annals* (p. 308) that
"women are publicly whipt for having an illegitimate
child" (1717). And it is interesting to read that Robert
J. Turnbull, of South Carolina, after describing his
visit to the prison at Philadelphia in 1797, makes a
special plea for the more humane treatment of "those
mothers who had not made public the death of their
illegitimate child." He continues by a statute of James
I: "concealment of the death of a bastard child is
made conclusive Testimony of its having been murdered
by the mother. No wonder that we should hear of a
female even applying to the horrid resource of murder-
ing an infant whose life is of little value when the
arrows of public infamy are in all circumstances darted
without distinction, and without recollecting that while
they may measure justice to the abandoned prostitute
they fail not to pierce at times the most virtuous bosom.
Shame to the sentiment which involves in the vortex
of vice every obedience to natural impulse, not immediately clothed with the garb and sanction of matri-
mony."

Appendix IV

THE WALKING PURCHASE

"A council was held with the Delaware Indians at Philadelphia, August 24th, 1737, at which was present 'The Hon'ble Thomas Penn, Esq., Prop'r,' and others" (*Pennsylvania Archives*, vol. i, pp. 539-543). Thomas Penn later denied his presence at this convened assembly, but further details given of the same meeting, record that he had consultation with his own colleagues and then a discourse with the Indian representatives concerning a proposed purchase of land by a 'walk.'[1] Both parties considered and approved the plan, agreed to the time when the event should take place and marked out the boundary lines which Penn knew, but which the Indians had to take on trust. Their interpreter stated that they were "desirous to preserve and continue the same love and friendship that had subsisted between William Penn and all the Indians, and presented a belt of wampum to Thomas Penn adding that they should be sorry if, after this mutual love and Friendship, anything should arise that might create the least misunderstanding, which they will carefully endeavour to avoid." This method of purchase had been used previously by William Penn with mutual confidence and satisfaction. White men and Indians walked and had a happy time together, journeying leisurely in friendly manner, so that a reasonable

[1] For a full account see W. J. Buck, *History of the Indian Walk* (Philadelphia, 1886) from which the facts here cited are derived.

distance was covered in a given time, and therefore purchased. But Thomas Penn did not work in this amicable way. He misled the Indians by making another boundary line *parallel with the Delaware*, instead of representing it as it should have been, further north. A Trial Walk, held two years previously, had indicated where the line ought actually to have been. Penn also hired a sprinter who tricked the Indians as to the distance covered, and then he produced a spurious 'Deed' supposed to have been drawn up in 1686 with the Indians' signatures to it, and quoting that Deed (although he could not produce the original) presumed land to be already purchased which never had been. Deeds of release of lands in 1718 were produced by the Indians, showing their transactions with William Penn, but these were utterly ignored. That there was every intent to deceive the Indians, on the part of Thomas Penn, there is ample proof in the records of his own writings. He instructed his men to find "that man of the three which travelled and held out the best when they walked over the land before to attend to that service at the time mentioned." A bribe of 500 acres was offered to one, Edward Marshall, if he should perform the task in such a manner as to beat the Indians and so obtain the greatest area of purchase. Two other athletes were selected and the Indians chose their own three competitors, with supervisors to see that all was fair. But during the twenty-four days between the drafting of the release and the actual event, the hired men of Thomas Penn tried out the ground and found the easiest paths to travel. In so doing they deviated from the route mapped out and agreed upon.

Those present at the Walk have given an account of

this infamous affair in writing "to the King and Government of Great Britain" in order to ascertain the cause of the Indian wars "and the alleged abuses and misconduct of the Penns in the colony." From the outset there was an under current of feeling that the white men were outwitting the Indians. The riders who accompanied the walkers report that complaints were made frequently by the Indians: the English were so very eager to get a great distance covered that the slower ones sometimes had to run to catch the front men: they all three hurried at the last lap on the first day, to the top of a hill which they reached in a state of complete exhaustion. Overnight the horses strayed, a further cause of irritation, and much time was lost in recapturing them. As the Walk proceeded some dropped out from weariness and much dissatisfaction was evident: neither the manner of it, nor the path of it, nor the map of it was really just. The whole unworthy project was engineered by Thomas Penn alone: even those who took part in the actual experiment admit that the Indians were cheated. Edward Marshall, who did not even get a reward from the mean hand of his employer, and who had to pay a terrible penalty in the loss of wife and son, slain by vengeful and resentful Indians, maintained "to his latest breath that the Indians had been grossly wronged by the government of the Penns." Not satisfied with the achieved purchase by the Walkers, Penn diverted the line of boundary from a straight line to a line at right angles to the Delaware, again adding more territory to his rightful area. The surveyor-general had to record these districts by marking various trees, and drawing the traverse lines. When this was completed he found that it took *four days* to cover what the sprinter in the Walk had completed *in a day and a half.*

After the performance of the Walk, Thomas Penn sent a letter dated October 11th, 1737, to his brothers in England in which he says: "Since I wrote you last, I have at no very great expense concluded with the Delaware Indians on the Foot of the Agreement made in 1686, and with their consent the land in the upper part of Bucks County has been measured by walking a day and a half's journey, which though done to their satisfaction takes in as much ground as any person here ever expected." "Most of the Assembly," says Samuel Preston, "and many other judicious persons thought the whole affair a species of gambling worse than horse-racing, and threatened the peace of the country. . . . The Indians felt themselves much aggrieved by this unfair admeasurement of their lands; it was the cause of the first dissatisfaction between the Indians and the people of Pennsylvania; and it is remarkable that the first murder committed by them in the province, seventy-two years after the landing of Penn, was on this very ground which had been taken from them by fraud."

LIST OF WORKS CONSULTED

BRAILSFORD, M. R. *The Making of William Penn*. Longmans, London, 1930. *William Penn*. Friends' Tract Association, 1934.

BUCK, W. J. *William Penn in America*. Philadelphia, 1888. *The Indian Walk*.

BUELL, AUGUSTUS C. *William Penn as the Founder of Two Commonwealths*, 1904. By permission of D. Appleton-Century Co., Inc., owners of the copyright.

CARPENTER, HELEN. *The Trial of Philippe Vernier*. Translation from the *Cahiers de la Reconciliation*. H. Roser. Friends' Peace Committee, 1933.

CHALKLEY, THOMAS. *Collected Works*. London, 1766.

CLARKSON, THOMAS. *Memoirs of the Public and Private Life of William Penn*. 1849.

CUSHING, WILLIAM. *Anonyms: Dictionary of Revealed Authorship*. 1890.

DIXON, WILLIAM HEPWORTH. *History of William Penn—Founder of Pennsylvania*. 1872.

DOBRÉE, BONAMY. *William Penn—Quaker and Pioneer*. Constable, London, 1932.

DOYLE, J. A. *The Middle Colonies*. Longmans, London, 1907.

Encyclopædia Britannica, 11th Edition. Articles on "Penn"; "Pennsylvania"; "Indians, North American"; etc.

FRANKLIN, BENJAMIN. *An Historical Review of Pennsylvania*. 1759.

GRAHAM, J. W. *William Penn*. Allen & Unwin, London, 1916.

GREGG, RICHARD B. *The Power of Non-violence*. Routledge, London, 1936.

HAZARD, SAMUEL. *Register of Pennsylvania*.

HIRST, MARGARET. *The Quakers in Peace and War*. Allen & Unwin, London.

HOWARD, JOHN. *State of the Prisons*. 1784.

JANNEY, SAMUEL M. *The Life of William Penn*. Philadelphia, 1882.

JONES, RUFUS M. *Quakers in the American Colonies*. Macmillan, London, 1911.

KELSEY, RAYNER WICKERSHAM. *Friends and the Indians*. Philadelphia, 1917.

LEARNED, M. D. *Life of Francis Daniel Pastorius*. Philadelphia, 1908.

OAKLEY, VIOLET. *The Holy Experiment*. Philadelphia, 1922.

PENN, WILLIAM. *Collected Works*. London, 1726. *Letters to the Society of Traders*.

PROUD, ROBERT. *History of Pennsylvania*. Philadelphia, 1797.

SCHOOLCRAFT, HENRY R. *Notes on the Iroquois*. Albany, 1847.

SHARPLESS, ISAAC. *A Quaker Experiment in Government*. Alfred J. Ferris, Philadelphia, 1898. *The Quakers in Pennsylvania* (Book V of *The Quakers in the American Colonies*).

STOUGHTON, JOHN. *William Penn—The Founder of Pennsylvania*. London, 1882.

THOMAS, GABRIEL. *An Account of Pennsylvania*. 1698.

TURNBULL, ROBERT J. *A visit to the Philadelphia Prison*. Philadelphia, 1797.

VULLIAMY, C. E. *William Penn*. Geoffrey Bles, London, 1933.

WALTON, JOSEPH S. *Conrad Weiser and the Indian Policy of Colonial Pennsylvania*. Philadelphia, 1900.

WATSON, J. F. *Annals of Philadelphia*. 1844.

WINSOR, JUSTIN. *The Mississippi Basin: The Struggle in America between England and France, 1697-1763*. Houghton Mifflin Company, Boston. 1895.

INDEX

PRINTED BY THE STANHOPE PRESS LTD., ROCHESTER, KENT